Developing Core Competence Through Multicultural Learning

Rasoava Rijamampianina

Universal Publishers
1999

Copyright © 1999 Rasoava Rijamampianina
All rights reserved.

ISBN: 1-58112-874-6

Universal Publishers/UPUBLISH.COM
1999

www.upublish.com/books/rija.htm

Acknowledgements

The author is grateful to many people. The managers and employees of Kraomita Malagasy (KRAOMA) and STAR-Madagascar (STAR) kindly responded to my questionnaires. The managers and employees of Ericsson Toshiba Telecommunication System K.K. kindly received me for interviews and shared their experiences with me. The Japanese Government, through its Ministry of Education, funded the research and conferences, which resulted in this book. Professor Yoshiya Teramoto was generous with advice, perspective, and encouragement. Professor Hiromitsu Kojima, Professor Kazuyori Kanai, Professor Shigeo Kuroda, Professor Yasuki Sekiguchi, and Associate Professor Hiromichi Shibata provided their academic comments. Brian R. Blevens granted a generous portion of his time, as he assisted with technical help. Furthermore, I appreciate the unique contributions of my wife, my son, my parents, and my mother-in-law. Finally, I am grateful to others who collaborated with me in one way or another and made this book possible.

Rasoava RIJAMAMPIANINA, D.B.A.

Contents

ACKNOWLEDGEMENTS I

1. DARE TO BE DIFFERENT 1

1.1. UNDENIABLE REASONS 1
1.1.1. Facts and Realities 1
1.1.2. Gaps in Prior Studies 2
1.2. RESULTING PURPOSES OF THIS BOOK 5
1.3. GOLDEN DIFFERENCES 5

2. DARE TO BE ACCURATE 7

2.1. CULTURE 7
2.1.1. Reviewing the Concept of Culture 7
2.1.2. Culture Does Matter 10
2.2. CULTURAL DIVERSITY 11
2.2.1 Reviewing the Concept of Cultural Diversity 11
2.2.2. Toward a Scientific Approach of Measuring Cultural Diversity 14
2.2.3. Influences of Cultural Diversity on Management ... 16
2.2.4. Toward a Scientific Approach of Measuring the Effects of Cultural Diversity on the Workplace Environment, the Management, and the Organizational Performance 26
2.3. LIMITS AND PROBLEMS OF PRIOR CONCEPTS 27
2.3.1. The Concept of "Divide and Rule" 27
2.3.2. The Concept of "Melting Pot" 28
2.3.3. The Concept of "Salad Bowl" 29
2.3.4. The Concept of Cross-cultural Interface Management 29
2.4. CORE COMPETENCE AND ORGANIZATIONAL LEARNING 32
2.4.1. The Concept of Core Competence 32
2.4.2. Anatomy and Evolution of Core Competence 34

2.4.3. The Linkage between Organizational Learning
and Core Competence 35

3. DARE TO BE EFFECTIVE 36

3.1. DEFINITION OF MULTICULTURAL MANAGEMENT ... 36
3.2. MODEL FOR AN EFFECTIVE MULTICULTURAL
MANAGEMENT 36
    3.2.1. Toward Success Sharing 37
    3.2.2. Toward Mental Models Sharing 43
    3.2.3. Toward Vision Sharing 54
    3.2.4. Toward Core Competence Development 56
    3.2.5. Toward Co-success 61
3.3. SPECIFIC HYPOTHESES 62
    3.3.1. Effects of Cultural Distances 62
    3.3.2. Conditions for an Effective Multicultural
    Management 65
    3.3.3. Linkage Between Core Competence Development
    and Performance 70

4. STANDING IN THE GAP 71

4.1. QUANTITATIVE STUDY 71
    4.1.1. Questionnaire for the Management 71
    4.1.2. Questionnaire for the Employees 72
4.2. CASE STUDY 77
    4.2.1. Purpose and Design of the Interview 77
    4.2.2. Contents of the Interview 77
    4.2.3. Process of the Interview 77

5. QUANTITATIVE ANALYSIS:
THE CASES OF KRAOMA & STAR 79

5.1. PRESENTATION OF MADAGASCAR 79
    5.1.1. Geographical Situation 79
    5.1.2. Population and Cultures 79
    5.1.3. Historical Background 83
    5.1.4. Madagascarian Organizations 87

5.2. PRESENTATION OF THE COMPANIES................... 87
   5.2.1. Kraomita Malagasy (KRAOMA) 87
   5.2.2. Star-MADAGASCAR (STAR) 94
5.3. KRAOMA.. 101
   5.3.1. Responses to Questionnaires 101
   5.3.2. The Sampled Employees 101
   5.3.3. Measurement of Cultural Diversity 102
   5.3.4. Hypotheses Testing 108
   5.3.5. Interpretations, Findings, and Discussions 137
5.4. STAR... 146
   5.4.1. Responses to Questionnaires 146
   5.4.2. The Sampled Employees 146
   5.4.3. Measurement of Cultural Diversity 148
   5.4.4. Hypotheses Testing 153
   5.4.5. Interpretations, Findings, and Discussions 185
5.5. SUMMARY: A COMPARISON OF THE TWO STUDIED
COMPANIES.. 193
   5.5.1. Similarities... 193
   5.5.2. Differences.. 196

6. CASE ANALYSIS:
THE CASE OF ERICSSON TOSHIBA 199

6.1. THE FIRM'S OUTLINE 199
6.2. THE FIRM'S WORKFORCE 200
6.3. THE FIRM'S CORE COMPETENCE 201
6.4. THE THIRD GROUP'S STRATEGIC FUNCTIONS 202
6.5. THE NEW CONCEPT
      OF CONTEXTUAL SWITCHING............................ 207

7. CONCLUDING & FURTHER THOUGHTS 210

7.1. CONCLUSION 210
7.2. IMPLICATIONS 211
   7.2.1. Theoretical Implications 211
   7.2.2. Managerial Implications 212
7.3. FURTHER RESEARCH...................................... 214

REFERENCES 215

**APPENDIX: INDICATORS OF THE SELECTED
CULTURAL DIMENSIONS** 231

Chapter 1
DARE TO BE DIFFERENT

1.1. Undeniable Reasons

1.1.1. Facts and Realities

Beyond the significant number of multicultural countries, which are already widely recognized, today, we are living in a world where borders are decreasing in importance. People are moving from one place to another for economic, political, or social reasons rather than accepting the status quo in their environments. *Multicultural workforces* are therefore rapidly and irreversibly becoming the norm in a large number of organizational situations. Unfortunately, this fact nowadays is claimed to influence *negatively* organizational performance.

In addition, it is actually recognized that *global business* is on the rise. Almost all large companies now view themselves as members of both domestic and world communities, and literally every developed country is giving high priority to helping their small and medium-size businesses operate internationally. Nevertheless, reliance on domestic business or a shift toward international business operations is actually fraught with growth complexity, geographic distances, and cultural diversity.

In other words, the dramatic changes, which are occurring around the world, are not only due to the rapid changes in technology and new service opportunities, but also from the evolution of *new domestic infrastructures* and *competitive environments*.

Common agreements are therefore necessary across borders because there is a clear mutuality of interests, which would provide a significant incentive for compliance. That is why, actually, nations and organizations are more attracted to multicultural and international connections. Multicultural and international connections suppose global networking—that is, global mission, global vision, global markets, and interdependence on a global economy. Almost every theory of organizations presumes a tendency for environmental change to be reflected in organizational change. As a result, the era of intensifying global competition predicts that a firm's survival will depend less than previously on access to material resources or markets and more on how it can continuously learn and develop its strength—that is, its core competence. What is not known, however, is *how* a multicultural organization can be effectively managed so that it would be able to learn continuously and, thereby, develop its core competence. The synthesis and replenishment of the diverse competencies of a multicultural workforce and the mediation between diverse occupational values require new kinds of strategies in managing organizational forces.

1.1.2. Gaps in Prior Studies

Though the great challenge facing management might be described as *the search of HOW*, prior studies fall far short of providing practical guidance for managing the culturally diverse groups for at least ten (10) reasons:
1. *Case studies bear little resemblance to real life.* Most researchers have used short-term groups that existed only for the duration of their studies (e.g., Cox et al., 1991; Kirchmeyer and Cohen, 1992; Watson and Kumar, 1992; Watson et al., 1993). Their findings therefore give no guidance as to what to expect in ongoing organizational groups.
2. *Sample sizes fall below conventional levels* because organizations are reluctant to participate (Cox, 1990).
3. *There exists little empirical literature on the dynamics of culturally diverse work groups and even less on the*

effective management of such groups, though:
- ✧ Comparative studies have shown that culture affects the work-related values and behaviors of its members (e.g., Hofstede, 1984; McCarrey, 1988);
- ✧ The differences between cultures can cause difficulties in the multicultural workplace (e.g., Tang and Kirkbride, 1986; Vaid-Raizada, 1985).

4. *There has been little empirical research* on:
   - ✧ The notion of core competence;
   - ✧ The linkage between organizational learning and core competence;
   - ✧ Multicultural learning;

   while most of the empirical research on competencies within firms were much earlier (e.g., Hitt and Ireland, 1985, 1986; Snow and Hrebiniak, 1980).

5. *The tasks employed have been either quite simplistic* (Fenelon and Megargee, 1971) and/or *have had a game-like quality* (Ruhe and Allen, 1977), *having no significant impact on group members' well-being,* so that the relevance of the studies have been limited.

6. *The existing studies' conclusions are incongruent:*
   - ✧ Some studies concluded that racial diversity inhibited group performance (Fenelon and Mergagee, 1971; Ruhe and Allen, 1977); some found no performance differences between racially diverse and racially homogeneous groups; and some concluded that racial diversity enhanced groups' performance (Ruhe and Eatman, 1977; Watson et al., 1993).
   - ✧ Some specialists in this field argue that national or regional culture is rarely present in the firms (Maurice et al., 1980, 1992; Amadieu, 1993) or that it is often overpowered by organizational culture (Ivanier, 1992). The idea has been widespread that

organizational culture moderates or erases the influence of national or regional culture. It assumed that employees working for the same organization even if they are from different countries or regions are more similar than different (Adler, 1991). On the contrary, others affirm that national or regional culture is predominant compared with organizational culture (D'Iribarne, 1986; Hofstede, 1980; Laurent, 1983; Meschi and Roger, 1994).

7. *The greater the need for comparison, the greater the need to reduce complexity* (Evers, 1991). But consequently, though these analyses serve as useful background information, they are ineffective as recommendations for action.
8. *Scientifically, it is hard.* Indeed, ideally, we want to emphasize on the interactions among the cultures, given a host of other variables in a dynamic system. But much past research went awry because it mixed up culture as an outcome variable, as a causal variable, and as an indexer of utility functions. Moreover, the development of applied cultural studies faces grave difficulties in:
    ✧ Defining variables
    ✧ Data collection
    ✧ Empirical estimation
9. *It is no longer easy to determine one specific set of objective leadership standards* that the "good manager" can put into practice to be successful. Relativity and flexibility are the new norms (Simons et al., 1993).
10. *A warranted fear of misuse and misunderstanding.* The possible contribution to stereotyping and dynamic effects on group identities reveals that considering culture touches on sensitive questions. These questions are: what are our purposes and what it means, "to analyze a culture" with intellectual inquiry as well as on a philosophical level?

1.2. Resulting Purposes of this Book

The purposes of this book are therefore:
- To address the real and practical issues and improvements of cultural diversity in management with empirical data and case analysis.
- To offer a practical and effective strategy of promoting non-dominant cultures and better mixing up management rank, while ensuring optimal performance and maintaining a skilled workforce, which would be willing and able to continuously learn and develop the firm's core competence.

1.3. Golden Differences NEW

1. *Optimistic view of cultural diversity.* Prior studies hypothesize that cultural diversity is difficult to manage and to coordinate. However, it could also bring some *positive effects* if heterogeneous energies, viewpoints, ways of doing and thinking, skills, and so on, are effectively integrated. The uniqueness of this book would therefore stem from the way of viewing cultural diversity as an originator of a dynamic situation.
2. *New concepts: multicultural learning and dynamic core competence.* As a consequence of the first point, this book will offer:
    - The concept of multicultural learning as a driving force for core competence development;
    - The concept of dynamic core competence based on continuous multicultural learning and development of core competence;
    - The concept of motivational, interaction, visioning, and learning processes into systems frameworks. This, hopefully, would not change only the organizational members' numbers and attitudes but

also the way an organization is managed.
3. *Empirical research and work-related case analysis on multicultural learning and dynamic core competence.* In order to overcome some of the above mentioned gaps in previous research, this book will:
    - Be based on real and work-related cases and will therefore attempt to provide management a practical way to:
        - Balance multicultural workforce's representation and power without replacing one dominant group with another;
        - Create a willingness-to-share environment that would welcome and foster multicultural learning and, thereby, core competence development;
        - Understand and utilize the great asset—cultural diversity—in more suitable and productive positions and at their highest potentials.
    - Attempt to address the issues of cultural diversity with empirical data and a further case study.
4. *Broader scope of study.* Though prior studies usually tend to confine their analyses to the cases of Japan vs. U.S. or Japan vs. U.K. or Japanese multinationals operating in the U.S. or in Europe (everything at the national level), this book will attempt to offer a broader scope of study by analyzing:
    - Cultural diversity, both at the national and the ethnic groups levels;
    - Malagasy companies (local companies) and a foreign multinational company operating in Japan.

Chapter 2
DARE TO BE ACCURATE

2. 1. Culture

2. 1. 1. Reviewing the Concept of Culture

From a narrow perspective, *culture* could be defined as "...that complex of activities which includes the practice of the arts and of certain intellectual disciplines, the former being more salient than the latter" (Trilling, 1978). Most management researchers subscribe to a view of culture which sees it as a set of ideas shared by members of a group (e.g. Allaire and Firsirotu, 1984). Culture is therefore not an individual characteristic but rather denotes a set of common theories of behavior or mental programs (Hofstede, 1980, 1984, 1994) that are shared by a group of individuals.

Harris and Moran (1987) define culture as "the cumulative deposit of knowledge, beliefs, values, religion, customs, and mores acquired by a group of people and passed on from generation to generation. It includes not only arts and letters, but also ways of lives, values systems, traditions, and beliefs."

Majority of cultural components (e.g., beliefs, values, norms, perceptions, attitudes, and priorities) is less visible (Kotter and Heskett, 1992; Schein, 1992), which makes them more difficult to understand and cope with successfully. Therefore, culture could be viewed as a group of hidden and recurring patterns of behavior and thought. According to Aviel (1990) and Cushner and Trifonovitch (1989), they are hidden because individuals learn to behave appropriately in a given culture and little conscious thought is given to the actual behaviors and how those behaviors are learned.

This is consistent with Kohls's (1981) definition that "culture is an integrated system of learned behavior patterns that are characteristic of the members of any given society. It includes everything that a group thinks, says, does, and makes—its customs, language, material artifacts, and shared systems of attitudes and feelings."

Kotter and Heskett (1992) state that, at the deeper and less visible level, culture refers to values that are shared by the people in a group and that tend to persist over time even when group membership changes. At the more visible level, culture represents the group's behavior patterns or style. At this level, culture is thought to change, not nearly as difficult as at the level of basic values.

In any given culture, some values are regarded as more important than others. And in different cultures, the relative importance attributed to particular values may differ (e.g., Kluckhohn and Strodtbeck, 1961; Rokeach, 1973). Within a culture, values are organized in a hierarchy or a relative order of priority. The terms **"Core"** and **"Periphery"** may therefore be used to represent, respectively, the relatively high and the relatively low positioning of values in the values hierarchy and the extent to which they are involved in social control (Lachman et al., 1994).

Many of the prior studies, however, do not consider (see Figure 1):
- The interrelationship between cultural visibility and centrality of values;
- The interrelationship of cultural visibility and centrality of with conflict in intercultural interactions.

Hence, the definition that best suits the reality and the scope of this study would be as follows:

> *"Culture is created, acquired and/or learned, developed, and passed on by a group of people, consciously or unconsciously, to subsequent*

generations. It includes everything that a group thinks, says, does, and makes—its customs, ideas, mores, habits, traditions, language, material artifacts, and shared systems of attitudes and feelings—that help to create standards for people to coexist."

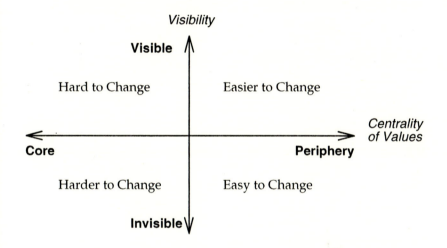

Figure 1: The structure of individuals' cultures

This definition encompasses a wide variety of elements from the visible to the invisible, from the core values to the periphery values, and embraces both national, regional, and ethnic boundaries.

Figure 1 shows that values higher in the hierarchy—that is, core values—are more important, more enduring and resistant to change, mainly if they are invisible (e.g., Americans give primary value to freedom and independence; and Arabs highly value religious belief and devotion). They are highly accepted within a cultural group, thus, are more likely to cause conflict in intercultural interactions. Resistance to change softens when core values are becoming visible (e.g., Elashmawi and Harris

[1993] say that the new generation in Japan is now putting more priority on self-reliance as opposed to the older generation, which valued belonging to a group).

Values of low priority, low consensus, and less importance—that is, periphery values—are on the contrary relatively susceptible to change (Shils, 1961). They are more easily subject to change when they are visible (e.g., clothing, housing) than when they are not.

2.1.2. Culture Does Matter

Traditionally, organizations were managed with *an ethnocentric approach to culture*, which assumes that any society has the same basic values and goals that characterize Western countries. But the evidence to date shows that this assumption is not valid. Although the concept of culture is difficult to define in practice, it is widely accepted that culture has significant effects on organizations (Bhagat and MacQuaid, 1982; Denison, 1990). Culture differs in any society or social group and it does matter.

To better analyze this question, consider the following simplified equations:

(1) Utility$_{Ci}$ = U$_{Ci}$(Performance, Management, Environment...)
(2) Performance = P (Management, Environment, Culture...)
(3) Culture = C (Performance, Management, Environment...)

Equation (1) indicates that the social utility function under cultural conditions Ci has many dimensions such as, performance, management style, environmental conditions broadly construed, and so on. The functional form of the utility function depends on the cultural conditions (e.g., Carnevale and Stone, 1994; Cox, 1991, 1993; Wilhelm, 1994), including the possibility of diverse arguments in varied cultures (e.g., Cox et al., 1991; Maznevski, 1994; McLeod and Lobe, 1992; Watson et al., 1993).

Equation (2) states that performance is a function of management style applied, the environment broadly construed, cultural variables (e.g., Carnevale and Stone, 1994; Fershtman and Weiss, 1993; Weber, 1977), and so on.

Equation (3) suggests that the cultural vector itself is a function of many factors including performance (e.g., Baker, 1994; Simons et al., 1993), management choices (e.g., Kirchmeyer and Cohen, 1992; Maznevski, 1994; Tjosvold, 1991), environmental conditions, and so on. This equation suggests that culture is not static but subject to change. Some of these changes are planned and many are unplanned; some can be prevented or retarded or advanced and others cannot.

With such equations, how could decisions be made? The manager's instinct is to choose a management style to maximize utility, taking cultural conditions and other variables into account. But the equations show that the maximization problem would be a complicated one indeed. Especially, if you look at "Culture". It is, at the same time, a dependent variable in equation (3), an independent or moderating variable in equation (2), and a giver of meaning in equation (1), in the sense that the utility function itself depends to some degree on the culture. In making choices, culture should be considered in all these ways. With such knowledge in hand, the type of management with *new horizons*—that is, with cultural variables—could be rethought.

2.2. Cultural Diversity

2.2.1 Reviewing the Concept of Cultural Diversity

Culture group or cultural group refers to an affiliation of people who collectively share certain norms, values, or traditions that are different from those of other groups.

According to Cox (1993), "cultural diversity therefore means the representation, in one social system, of people with distinctly different group affiliations of cultural significance."
In addition, Cox assumes that a majority group and a number of minority groups generally characterize the contexts of social systems. Majority group means the largest group, while minority group means a group with fewer members represented in the social system compared to the majority group. And in *most* social systems, one group may be identified both larger in size and as possessing greater power and economic advantages.

Mazrui (1992) however views societies into three categories:
1. *Homogeneous* society, in which over 80% of the population are in the same cultural tradition. A homogeneous has a minimum of multiculturalism.
2. *Preponderant* society, in which just over 50% belong to the same cultural tradition.
3. *Heterogeneous* society, in which no cultural group is close to 50% of the population. Usually this is the most multicultural.

That is, it is a homogeneous social system with a minimum multiculturalism, which is more probable to be characterized by majority group and minority groups than a heterogeneous one. Moreover, though Cox (1993) and Mazrui (1992) both consider all social systems being culturally diverse, Mazrui argues that the degrees of diversity are different depending upon the proportions of the cultural groups within the social systems.

In this book, it is argued that:

> "*Cultural diversity, as it is understood in the workplace today, implies differences in people based on their identifications with various cultural groups. However, cultural diversity is not only defined by the number or proportion of cultural groups within the social system but also*

by the significance of their cultural distance[1]."

In other words, disregarding the number or proportion of cultural groups[2] in a given social system:
- If the cultural distances between the existing cultures are not significant, the social system could be viewed as homogeneous, thus, cannot be said to be multicultural.
- If the cultural distances between the existing cultures are significant, the social system can be said to be multicultural, because the diversity is then relevant.

Cultural distances may be due to various factors [e.g., gender, differences in race, in nationality, in age, in educational level, in occupational level, in religion, and so on (Hofstede, 1994)]. It is therefore misleading to state that cultural diversity is caused by a single factor, though indeed, one factor may be more significant than the others.

In addition, a majority group is not always necessarily the dominant group. Therefore, in order to better generalize the analysis and to avoid any confusion or controversy about the relationships between the cultural groups' sizes and their power and advantages (that is, opportunity to succeed), from here, the following terms will be used throughout the book:
- *Dominant groups:* which means, the groups who hold the power and economic resources;
- *Non-dominant groups:* that is, the other groups.

---

[1] **Cultural Distance**, a correlative term, refers to the amount of difference in average scores on specific dimensions of culture content (Cox, 1993).
[2] Cultural diversity supposes the existence of more than two cultural groups.

2.2.2. Toward a Scientific Approach of Measuring Cultural Diversity

Beyond the above mentioned gaps in prior studies (Section 1.1.2.), to date, cultural distances between countries and ethnic groups were measured by just comparing the amount of differences in average scores on specific dimensions of culture content[3].

In other words, prior researchers rather cared about the average score differences in absolute values than the significance of these differences. Such approach is however very misleading in the sense that:
- As it was mentioned earlier, culture is by fact a function of core, periphery, invisible, and visible values (Figure 1);
- Differences in average score may include visible and periphery values (values of low priority, low consensus, and less importance, easily subject to change).

---

[3] Hofstede's (1980) and some of Kluckhohn and Strodtbeck's (1961) dimensions have been commonly used by numerous prior researchers.

Power distance (PD): defines the extent to which a group of people feels and perceives unequal distribution of power in institutions and organizations.

Uncertainty avoidance (UA): defines the extent to which people in a culture feel threatened by uncertainty and ambiguous situations and try to avoid such situations.

Masculinity orientation (MO): indicates the extent to which the dominant values of a group of people are "masculine" (e.g., assertion, competition, self-achievement, and so on).

Group orientation (GO): implies a tightly knit social framework in which the "in-groups" are expected to take care of their members.

Task orientation (TO): indicates the extent to which the dominant values of a group of people are task related.

Space orientation (SO): defines the extent to which the dominant values of a group of people are space related.

Human relation orientation (HR): indicates the extent to which the dominant values of a group of people are human relation related.

Prior studies like that of Hofstede's (1980, 1984, 1991, 1994) assume a static environment where cultural dimensions such as power distance and masculinity do not consider both the structure of cultures and the interactions which may influence these cultures. Hence, they based their analysis on a simple comparison of average scores.

This book therefore suggests that data would be analyzed with an interaction-based viewpoint since, in reality:
- Organizational environment is rather dynamic than static;
- Measurement of cultural diversity should:
  - Consider the structure of individuals' cultures within the dynamic environment;
  - Point out the significance of their cultural differences while considering the dynamic environment, which may shape some parts of their cultures.

Schematically, when a cultural distance has high absolute value but not significant, it would mean that the difference might incorporate a lot of visible and periphery values. On the contrary, though a cultural distance may have a low absolute value but is significant, it would indicate that the difference is composed of invisible and core values that are highly accepted within a cultural group, thus, they are more likely to cause conflicts in intercultural interactions.

Practically, with the ANOVA procedure within the SAS (Statistical Analysis System), for example, one could compare the cultural groups' average scores on specific dimensions of culture content. The multiple comparison methods within this procedure offer detailed information about the significance of the differences among the average scores and allow the control of error rates for a multitude of comparisons.

2.2.3. Influences of Cultural Diversity on Management

Since people's assumptions, beliefs, values, interests and needs, and goals are shaped by the culture to which they belong, they can be fairly deeply rooted in an individual. One should therefore assume, at least in the short run, that culture could not be changed to meet the demands of management. In the case of national or ethnic cultures, they are also usually supported by a complex and long-established social system, which has a vibrant existence outside the context of a business organization, fathering power and opportunity discrepancies between the cultural groups. Thus, one should take the position here that an individual's behavior in a organization will mainly be guided by the outside culture from which he/she comes (Jaeger, 1990).

Members of a multicultural organization therefore would not share a common set of assumptions, beliefs, values, interests and needs, nor goals, which originate from the local environment. Indeed, employees do not leave their cultures at the company's door when they come to work. Jaeger (1990) says that these cultural values from the environment are brought into the workplace and their differences would have a strong impact on the behavior of persons within the organization.

The practical impact of cultural diversity on management practices would therefore be identified in (Figure 2):
- *Motivational process,* because individuals in organizations would have various opportunities and interests and needs—these are the foundations of motivation;
- *Interaction process,* because members of organizations would not share a common set of assumptions; they would not perceive and evaluate attitudes and behaviors similarly, thus they would also act differently. Herein lies the source of miscommunication, misunderstanding, competitive or even destructive conflicts, disrespect, and mistrust;

- *Visioning process,* because visioning process could be only effectively achieved after the accomplishment of the motivational and interaction processes. That is, common needs and aspirations and goals (from the motivational process) would be needed in conjunction with a common way of seeing the world (from the interaction process). If these elements are found in combination, then there would be a sharing of vision.
- *Learning process,* because without a common vision, there would be no question of collective learning. Moreover, individuals in organizations would hold diverse experiences, varied ways of thinking and doing, and different knowledge;
- *Performance,* because work output would depend upon the above cited processes as a whole.

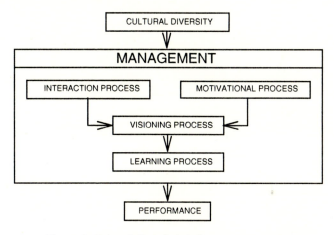

Figure 2: Cultural diversity's influences on management

The influences of cultural diversity on each of these processes will be accurately discussed in the following paragraphs[4].

2.2.3.1. Influences on Motivational Process

In summarizing the research on when and under which conditions everyone contributes in teams and benefits from differences, Slepian (1993) found that status and power differences could inhibit contributions.

When workgroups are diverse and the power distribution is heavily skewed in favor of a certain group or groups, it is more difficult for members of different culture groups to work harmoniously together and this may hamper organizational members' motivation. Indeed, these power discrepancies are a primary source of conflicts, Randolph and Blackburn (1989) affirm.

Most of non-dominant group members would be favorable to promote a redistribution of power in organizations, while many dominant group members would oppose it as an unwarranted and misguided policy of reverse discrimination (Cox, 1993). Cox asserts that imbalances, especially when they persist over a long period of time, have the effect of reducing the motivation and the perceived opportunity among members of non-dominant groups to participate and to excel to their fullest potential in diverse-group settings. Hence, the importance of seeking more balanced representation and power among culture groups in organizations.

It is noteworthy to mention however that *to balance*

---

[4] Though relationships may also exist between motivational and interaction processes and that upward relationships are imaginable, in this study, since the main objective is to show the strategy for an effective multicultural management through multicultural learning, looking at the *downward* arrows would be more interested.

representation and power is not attempting *to replace* one dominant group with another.

2.2.3.2. Influences on Interaction Process

Jaeger (1990) mentioned that members of a cultural group share complementary attitude and behavioral programs, which regulate their interaction. Associated with these programs are values and ideology, which provide a guide and a meaning to what they are doing and/or thinking. Thus, within a multicultural group, certain attitudes and behaviors will generate a feeling and response that is positive while others will generate a negative feeling and response.

- **Communication**

Communication is defined as "a process of circular interaction, which involves a sender, receiver, and message" (Harris and Moran, 1987). The sender or receiver may be one person or several people. Messages may be sent verbally or non-verbally. The way in which input is received and interpreted is influenced by an individual's culture. Therefore, two people can receive the same message and perceive two completely different meanings (Harris and Moran, 1987; Dorais, 1994).

A heightened incidence of communication difficulties has been associated with heterogeneous groups, including multicultural ones (Ruhe and Eatman, 1977; Triandis et al., 1965). Communication then can be discouraged when exchange predictability and attraction to the other are low (Triandis, 1960). People however cannot avoid communicating, because all human behavior communicates messages whether intended or not. Even if a person is completely silent, his/her body language will still communicate (Harris and Moran, 1987).

Because free and ongoing communication is an important

ingredient of creative problem solving (Ebadi and Utterback, 1984; Pelz and Andrews, 1978), overcoming the communication difficulties of multicultural work groups seems key to realizing the creative potential of such groups (Collins and Guetzkow, 1964; Shaw, 1981; Triandis et al., 1965).

- **Conflict**

Cultures vary in distinct and significant ways. Our ways of thinking, feeling, and behaving, as human beings are neither random nor haphazard, they are influenced by our cultural heritage. And because culture structures our expectations, assumptions and behavior, it is easy to see why cultural differences can lead to conflict. They make reaching agreement more difficult (Cox, 1991) and conflict occurs when the actions of one or more members of a group are incompatible with, and resisted by, one or more of the other group members. Conflicts also arise when members believe their different goals cannot be achieved simultaneously.

As a result, in practice, organizations typically aim to homogenize their multicultural work groups rather than attempt to use their inherent diversity (Brown, 1983; Fernandez, 1981; Jones, 1986).

However, conflict inevitably arises as a consequence of team functioning. Not only is conflict inevitable, but optimal team performance may require moderate levels of conflict. Without conflict, there may be no way to sense the need for change or draw attention to problem areas. Differences in values, orientations, and objectives may suggest different resolution strategies.

In brief, conflict can have negative and positive effects, depending upon its nature and amount, and how it is addressed (Gersick and Davis-Sacks, 1990). Conflict is unproductive when disagreements reach an impasse and incapacitate a team, but is useful when allowing team or organizational members to identify problems, develop learning and solutions, and work through tradeoffs without alienating members.

- **Mutual Understanding**

Cross-cultural understanding encompasses knowledge about how and why culturally different team-members act the way they do, and respect for differing cultural operating styles (Carnevale and Stone, 1994). Wilhelm (1994) states that cultural differences are one of the most common sources of professional misunderstanding. In his study on the influence of Mexican culture on the uses of American management theory in Mexico, he found that the Mexican perceives the Americans' directness as insensitive and cold-hearted, rather than efficient and professional. The US executive, who may sense an inability to get a straight answer from staff members, sometimes perceives this difficulty as reflecting dishonesty, inefficiency or lack of professionalism (Erlich, 1993).

People are often surprised to discover systematic differences in perceptions, but those differences are not a real shock. A real shock would be the absence of differences. All sorts of obstacles stand in the way of mutual understanding. Big differences in perception are the rule, Baker (1994) argues, not the exception. That is why managing relationships is difficult. Mutual understanding does not come naturally, you have to work at it.

- **Mutual Trust and Respect**

Trust, the mutual confidence that no party to an exchange will exploit the other's vulnerability, is today widely regarded as a precondition for success (Sabel, 1993). If trust is absent, no one will risk moving first, and all will sacrifice the gains of cooperation for the safe, less remunerative, autonomous pursuit of self-interest.

Cox (1993) however asserts that cultural differences create uncertainty about human behavior because when the cultural systems driving behavior are unknown, the behavior of others becomes less predictable.

What needs to be explained here is how the boundaries of a particular community are drawn or, collaterally, how mistrust rises. One way would be as the result of disputes that begin as disagreements (prompted, say, by the struggle for honor) over the interpretations of common norms, and end as the articulation of irreconcilable views of the world. Another would be as the result of the clashes of different cultural worlds which were, so to speak, irreconcilable from the first (Sabel, 1993).

The crucial point is that, there is nothing mysterious, in principle, about the creation of trust in teamwork and organizations. Trust can be created at will (Sabel, 1993). If the reflexive view of self and society is correct, then the real problem is how trust can be built in particular circumstances through a circuitous redefinition of collective values. It is only by recognizing their mutual dependence that the actors can define their distinct interests, and that government's role is to encourage the recognition of a collectivity and the definition of particularity.

- **Cooperation**

By definition, cooperation is working together for the mutual or common benefit of everyone involved. Thus, one could say that failure to cooperate for mutual benefit does not necessarily signal ignorance or irrationality (Sugden, 1986). Then, if engaging in cooperative behavior would increase every party's welfare, why would individuals not engage in cooperative behavior?

The problem of cooperation is not one of lack of knowledge of the opportunities and benefits of collaboration. Rather, it is a managerial problem of creating an environment in which people know their counterparts in other cultural groups or working group so well that collaboration—the bet that a favor given will be returned—represents a fair wager.

Moreover, Simons et al. (1993) states that cross-cultural

collaboration always and everywhere means changes on everybody's part. Working side by side, pursuing the same processes, and producing the same product always demands that people create a common way of thinking and viewing the world, which inevitably differs from that from which they came.

- **Mental Models**

The existence of mental models is widely asserted in the literature. According to Senge (1990, 1992), mental models can be simple generalizations, such as "people are untrustworthy," or they can be complex theories. But what is most important to grasp is that mental models shape how an individual acts. If one believes people are untrustworthy, he/she will act differently from the way others would if they believed people were trustworthy.

Mental models so powerfully affect what an individual does because, in part, they affect what he/she sees (Senge, 1990, 1992). Two people with different mental models can observe the same event and describe it differently because they have noticed different details (Carnevale and Stone, 1994).

In addition, sending my mental message through your mental framework may result in a distorted or totally different message than was intended (Simons et al., 1993). And in a workplace setting, such result may hamper individuals and/or groups' work relationships.

According to Senge (1990, 1992), the problems with mental models lie not in whether they are right or wrong (by definition), all models are simplifications. The problems with mental models arise when they exist below the level of awareness. When people remain unaware of their mental models, the models remain unexamined. And because they remain unexamined, they remain unchanged. So that, as the world changes, a gap widened between this people's mental models and reality, leading to increasingly counterproductive actions.

2.2.3.3. Influences on Visioning Process

Like other major organization changes, enhancing organizational capability to manage culturally diverse workforce should begin with creation of a vision that specifies, in broad terms, the objective of the change. The objective of managing a multicultural workforce should be to create organizations in which members of all socio-cultural backgrounds can contribute and achieve their full potential towards the vision.

Simons et al. (1993) however affirm that in a diverse workforce, not all people are so oriented. There are those who are oriented toward the present and are motivated by the quality of life they experience and those from more tightly knit cultures who look for continuity with the past. As a result, members of diverse groups generally have problems in agreeing on their purpose and on what tasks to perform.

Moreover, Cox (1993) states that in a multicultural social system, the various groups represented may develop different or even competing goals, which then become the basis of intergroup conflict. Cultural groups, teams, or organizational functions are also often characterized by very different systems of norms, goal priorities, work styles, and so on. In other words, they can be viewed as having different cultures. The difference in cultures between them, partly manifested in different goals, sets the stage for intergroup conflict.

Further, not everybody may perceive the goals the same way. Lack of goal unity or clarity reduces effectiveness (Larson and LaFasto, 1989).

2.2.3.4. Influences on Learning Process

During an interview made by Gosling (1994), Forbes asserted that "the languages are easy to handle. It is managing in a different culture, which has a different set of assumptions about effective management, which is the difficult learning curve."

It is actually spread that heterogeneity in workteams promotes creativity and innovation. Kanter's study of innovation in organization (1983), for example, revealed that the most innovative companies deliberately establish heterogeneous teams in order to create a marketplace of ideas, recognizing that a multiplicity of viewpoints need to be brought to generate/create ideas. Cox and Blake (1991) also reviewed studies that show that the use of differences leads to higher-quality group processes and products.

Learning organizations capitalize on differences because solutions often reside outside the norm. Teams are the playing ground on which differences can be used to question old ways of seeing things and to construct new knowledge (Marsick, 1994).

2.2.3.5. Influences on Performance

An important question for managing in the multicultural workplace asks how cultural diversity affects the performance of work groups.

Various avenues of research have suggested that an element of diversity serves as an important ingredient in creative problem solving. For example, experimental groups who were composed of members with unlike characteristics including ethnicity (Cox et al., 1991) outperformed groups of homogeneous members in terms of solution quality. Multicultural work groups offer numerous forms of diversity, including a diversity of values (Hofstede, 1984; McCarrey, 1988), one of cognitive structures (Redding, 1980), and another of behavioral styles (Jackofsky et al., 1988).

The potential productivity of culturally diverse teams is high because they have the additional breadth of insights, perspectives, and experiences that facilitate the creation of new and better ideas. The creative potential of multicultural work groups becomes an exciting notion, particularly in light of the current reality.

Regrettably, culturally diverse groups rarely achieve their full potential. Mistrust, misunderstanding, miscommunication, and so on often negate the potential benefits of diversity. Prior research (Copeland, 1988; Cox et al., 1991; Esty, 1988; Marmer-Solomon, 1989; Mandell and Kohler-Gray, 1990) recognizes that, only if well managed can culturally diverse teams hope to achieve their potential and overperform homogeneous ones. *"How to manage diversity"* is therefore a crucial question.

The solution has generally been to avoid using diverse groups whenever possible; however, because of the trends outlined above, this alternative is no longer feasible. Managers cannot allow the diversity to hinder performance, and furthermore they should be able to use diversity [to promote collective learning, thus,] to enhance performance (Maznevski, 1994).

2.2.4. Toward a Scientific Approach of Measuring the Effects of Cultural Diversity on the Workplace Environment, the Management, and the Organizational Performance

Usually, prior studies tend to assess the effects of cultural diversity on the workplace environment, the management, and the organizational performance by merely observing *pre-assumed* culturally heterogeneous and homogeneous groups working in teams (e.g., Cox et al. 1991; Fenelon and Mergagee, 1971; Ruhe and Allen, 1977).

To date, no scientific approach has been undertaken, so that:
- Only unrealistic and inconclusive results, that cause controversies and uncertainties, are still available;
- Prior studies fall for short of providing practical guidance for managing the culturally diverse groups.

Though some researchers (e.g., Evers, 1991) claim that it is scientifically hard to measure the interactions of various cultures in a dynamic system, today, numerous analytical tools are available to support a more scientific and realistic analysis. One of them is, for example, the CALIS procedure (Covariance Analysis of Linear Structural Equations) within the SAS package.

The CALIS procedure can be used to estimate parameters and hypotheses for constrained and unconstrained problems in:
✧ Multiple and multivariate linear regression;
✧ Linear measurement-error models;
✧ Path analysis and causal modeling;
✧ Simultaneous equation models with reciprocal causation;
✧ Exploratory or confirmatory factor analysis of any order;
✧ Canonical correlation;
✧ And so on...

2.3. Limits and Problems of Prior Concepts

2.3.1. The Concept of "Divide and Rule"

This is the oldest concept used to avoid cultural heterogeneity during the history plagued by foreign conquest or colonization. Thus, in contact between cultures, the colonizers tried to separate the various non-dominant groups, then, attempted to weaken and to destroy their cultures so that they would assimilate the new one (Wesseling, 1996).

This notion however felt short at the societal as well as at the

organizational levels because:
- The concept was just a one-way adaptation, thus, cultural exchange was minimal (Cox, 1993);
- The participants had to reject or at least repress the cultures from which they had come, so that many were unwilling or unable to adapt to the new culture and sought some autonomy from it (Berry, 1980; Cox and Finley-Nickelson, 1991);
- The notion was manifested in the segregation of members of non-dominant groups into certain job categories (Cox, 1993);
- A separation strategy was also pursued by the colonized people through voluntary isolation from members of the power structure of the society/organization in an effort to maintain some cultural autonomy (Cox, 1993).

2.3.2. The Concept of "Melting Pot"

The concept of a melting pot does not consider the possible existence of dominant and non-dominant cultures. It just gives the impression that the ingredients melt together and give up their identities to make one homogeneous product. In other words, the ultimate purpose is to form a "new homogeneous race" with a common culture.

This concept however failed because it ignored:
- The societal and organizational systems where, usually, one or some groups may be identified as possessing greater power and economic advantages than others (Cox, 1993);
- The above mentioned structure of individuals' cultures (Figure 1).

Not surprisingly, over the last two decades, it has been declared that the American melting pot ideal is dead (*Chicago Tribune*, March 8, 1990, p. 21). The reports of the demise of the melting pot indicated that the varied streams of American population could not undergo the ultimate form of smelting—intermarriage.

2.3.3. The Concept of "Salad Bowl"

The difference between the notion of the salad bowl and that of the melting pot is that, the salad bowl has a variety of ingredients, each of which maintains its own identity.

This concept also had been inefficient at the societal as well as at the organizational levels because:
- It only suggested simplicity;
- It did not consider the power of cultural diversity, thus, minimized the potential benefits of the culturally diverse individuals' integration.

2.3.4. The Concept of Cross-cultural Interface Management

According to Hayashi (1985, 1989), culturally mixed organizations are inevitable. Therefore, he proposes the concept of *cross-cultural interface management* to suggest corporate policies to alleviate strategic problems in multicultural organizations.

Cross-cultural interface refers to points of contact between cultures (Brown, 1983; Hayashi, 1985; 1989) and its central problems involve cross-cultural communication (Hayashi, 1985; 1989). Cross-cultural interface may be classified into:
- *Functional Interface,* which involves collaborative relations for specific objectives;
- *Non-functional Interface,* which may be found in one's relations with neighbors and with colleagues outside of work, that is, the contact is not designed to achieve predetermined objectives.

In Hayashi's (1985, 1989) studies, the firm's organization consists of (Figure 3):
1. Those who represent *the organizational culture of the main office* or FIRST CULTURE;
2. Those who embody *the local culture* or SECOND CULTURE;
3. Those who can *bridge* those two cultures or THIRD CULTURE.

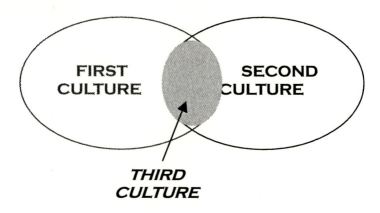

Figure 3: The cross-cultural interface structure

Brown (1983) views these elements as *cultural parties* and *cultural representatives* and he states that the existence of a cross-cultural interface must often be inferred from the relevance of cultural differences to conflict problems.

According to Hayashi (1985, 1989), the structure and management of cross-cultural interface are significant determinants of the firm's performance. Cross-cultural communications between the first and second cultures turn out to be the key factor. The first and the second cultures come into contact and it is *the interface administrator(s)* who bridge the two cultures, playing the role of *a boundary spanner*.

Interface administrators can serve as both[5]:
1. *Explainers,* to explicate to groups of the other culture the system of meanings (in general and the organizational cultures) to which they belong, in regard to business matters as they arise one after another.
2. *Interpreters,* on the basis of the system of meanings of the other culture, to decode the meanings of business matters as they arise one after another in the light of the system of meanings of their own general and organizational cultures.

There are flows of explanations and interpretations back and forth between the first and second cultures so that interface administrators begin to form **a third culture** which is a new system of knowledge, meanings, and values, as distinct from the first and second cultures (Figure 3).

The effectiveness of the interface administration depends upon:
- The scope of the interface;
- The amplitude and variety of cross-cultural contacts;
- The quality of explanations and interpretations.

---

[5] Therefore, requirements for an interface administrator are (Hayashi, 1985; 1989):
- Master of the first and second cultures' languages;
- Personal knowledge of the first and second cultures' knowledge, values, and meanings;
- Being trusted and/or legitimately a member of at least one of the two groups.

According to Brown (1983), almost any member of a cultural party may become a representative or interface administrator since potential cross-cultural contacts and conflicts are dispersed through the organization along with cultural differences. However, personal characteristics of interface administrators may be important to their ability to work at cross-cultural interface.

Hayashi's thought about cross-cultural interface management is interesting but the concept is basically confined to communications between two different cultures. However:
- The point is that it is not only a matter of communication, but also a matter of combining and integrating heterogeneous energies, viewpoints, ways of doing, ways of thinking, and competencies.
- Cultural diversity refers to the existence of more than two different cultures in the workplace. It is therefore very complex to use this concept within a multicultural organization.

Indeed:
➤ Being able to slip into and out of more than two cultures is a skill belonging to a limited number of individuals;
➤ The fulfillment of the requirements for an interface administrator would become very difficult and the scope of the interface would become larger and more complex.

2.4. Core Competence and Organizational Learning

2.4.1. The Concept of Core Competence

Many of the perspectives that dominated the early thinking concerning competitive advantage have their roots in traditional economic theory, with emphasis on market power and industry structure as determinants of performance (Caves, 1971; Caves and Porter, 1977; Chandler, 1990; Kogut, 1988; Porter, 1985; Rumelt, 1982, 1984; Williamson, 1985). They emphasize economies of scale and scope, the optimization of transaction costs across subsidiaries, and critical market characteristics to explain different firm-level strategies. In this theoretical context, firm strategies are designed to secure competitive advantage by responding to environmental changes and co-aligning firm strengths with external opportunities (Barney, 1991; Porter, 1985). Environmental conditions and industry characteristics are assumed to largely shape the firm's strategy.

In recent years, however, other streams of research emphasizing a "resource-based" or "skill-based" perspective of strategy and organization have evolved. They characterize the firm as a collection of unique skills and capabilities that influence the firm's evolution and strategic growth alternatives (Barney, 1991; Dierickx and Cool, 1989; Dosi, 1988; Itami, 1987; Mahoney and Pandian, 1992; Nelson and Winter, 1982; Wernerfelt, 1984; Winter, 1987). The resource-based approach suggests that differences in internal firm characteristics, such as idiosyncratic patterns of learning and asset (tangible and intangible) accumulation, have important effects on the firm's ability to develop new products and processes across disparate markets. Moreover, the same characteristics define firm heterogeneity through differences in strategy and learning potential. Consequently, how a firm nurtures and develops its unique set of resources and skills may be significant in determining its future strategies. Thus, a firm's competitive advantage is derived from its unique knowledge (Spender, 1993).

Evolving from the resource-based view is the concept of core competence. Herein, *Core Competence* will be simply:

> *"A set of competencies which can create and develop competitive advantages successively."*

This notion of core competence is consistent with the early studies on competencies (e.g., Hitt and Ireland, 1985, 1986; Snow and Hrebiniak, 1980).

Furthermore, core competence:
- ◆ Is not a single unit of competence. It is rather a set of competencies.

♦ Is developed from organizational learning.
♦ Should not be inertial. It should be subject to change through time. Hence the need to learn continuously. As such, this study's focus is on *dynamic core competence*.
♦ Should be kept within the organization, therefore it cannot and should not be outsourced.

2.4.2. Anatomy and Evolution of Core Competence

Today, it is widely recognized that, companies, which are able to develop core competence continuously (dynamism of core competence), can develop long-lasting competitive advantage (Teramoto et al., 1993a, 1993b). Therefore, beyond the creation of knowledge, firms should have power to develop core competence to face the new world order. That is, beyond potential exchanges of information, knowledge, experience, and skill, firms should also consider and foster core competence development and co-creation of new core competence.

This book would suggest that (Figure 4):
- *Information and Tacit Knowledge*[6] become *Experience* after practical acquaintance with it;
- *Experience* becomes *Codified Knowledge* when it can be transferred after its codification;
- *Codified Knowledge* becomes *Skill*[7] when it has been mastered through repetition, to improve the quality of the existing output;
- *Skill* becomes *Core Competence* when a higher social level recognizes the repeated outputs it generates.

---

[6] The argument here is that *Information* becomes *Tacit Knowledge* when it is understood and is likely to be used for a given purpose.
[7] In this paper, *Skill* is defined as a talent that can be transferred to other persons.

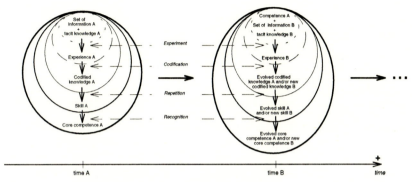

Figure 4: The anatomy and evolution of an individual's core competence

```
•{A, B, A < B;
set of information A •, set of information
   tacit knowledge A •, tacit knowledge B;
         experience A < experience B;
codified knowledge A < codified knowledge I
            skill A < skill B;
  core competence A < core competence B
```

2.4.3. The Linkage between Organizational Learning and Core Competence

Most approaches to organizational learning (e.g., Argyris and Schon, 1978; Hedberg, 1981; Huber, 1991) have assumed that learning was uninformed by a conscious firm strategy. By contrast, the early strategy literature suggested the importance of skills and competencies (Andrews, 1971; Ansoff, 1965) as the basis for selecting an appropriate strategy but failed to view these as learned or capable of development through further learning. More recent empirical work (e.g., Hitt and Ireland, 1985, 1986) continued with this implicit assumption. Alternatively, recent conceptual works have viewed competencies as dynamic and suggested the importance of organizational learning for their development (Fiol, 1991; Hamel, 1991; Reed and DeFillipi, 1990). However, there is need for a comprehensive and integrative model that shows the interrelationship between organizational learning and dynamic core competence. And here is the concern of the next chapter.

Chapter 3
DARE TO BE EFFECTIVE

3.1. Definition of Multicultural Management   NEW

Although within recent years, multicultural management has become a popular topic within management in general and organizational behavior and human resource management in particular, considerable confusion still exists as to what managing diversity actually is. In this book's definition,

> *"Managing cultural diversity means creating and/or promoting a multicultural learning-based order with a sharing principle so that everybody and the organization itself would be willing and able to develop core competence."*

Managing diversity, therefore, considers motivational, interaction, visioning, and learning processes simultaneously, and expands the notion of valuing diversity by implementing initiatives at all levels in an organization. The goal is to develop an environment that works for all employees (Thomas, 1990) and to maximize the potential benefits of diversity while minimizing the potential drawbacks (Cox, 1991).

3.2. Model for an Effective Multicultural Management

Since diversity in many situations is a fact of life and not a choice and since the potential benefits of diversity appear to be greater than the potential costs (Cox and Blake, 1991), the challenge for organization is to increase these benefits while decreasing the negative effects of diversity.

As a team, employees are the organization and will have to be treated differently than in the past. Managers will have to design new motivational, interaction, visioning, and learning strategies.

Management responsibility is therefore to provide necessary training and transparent performance evaluation feedback to:
- Promote an open and equal opportunity environment;
- Develop plans to share the work results with employees;
- Create an environment, which welcomes mental models sharing;
- Support vision creation with employees;
- Encourage core competence development.

The central point is establishing a learning attitude among workers so that their organization can learn. Without individual learning, team learning cannot occur; and without team learning, there can be no question of organizational learning (Swieringa and Wierdsma, 1992). In the new reality, without organizational learning, core competence development and performance improvement can be difficult to achieve, even impossible.

3.2.1. Toward Success Sharing

Just as macroeconomics can travel anywhere and be the same, there are also some universal management characteristics that can travel in the same manner. Management is, for example, universally about motivation[8] since people's needs and motives are remarkably universal. All employees, for example, have the need to feel productive, to participate in the

---

[8] Motivation can be defined as getting people to want to perform (Simons et al., 1993).

success sharing or, at least, to earn their pay. This desire to be successful in performing job duties and to share the outcomes motivates employees of all cultural backgrounds to master job skills and routines.

Teams are usually motivated to produce more and better ideas if all members have more or less equal power and opportunity to participate in the given activity. Managers should distribute power according to each member's ability to contribute to the task, not according to some preconceived notion of relative cultural superiority.

Organizations with team environments should therefore train teamwork as part of their development programs[9]. And in order to motivate teamwork in organizations with team environments, performance appraisals should be modified to assess and reward the behavioral and performance indicators of the teamwork.

The central point in this section is that without an open and equal opportunity environment, there can be no question of success sharing.

An open and equal opportunity environment can be realized by providing training to the employees and by developing and improving the performance evaluation feedback and transparency. When people share success, it has to be made clear that the success and promotion opportunities open to them are equal and linked to the quality of their outputs so that they can be committed to improving or at least maintaining their efforts.

---

[9] *Training* is "a planned process to modify [and/or improve] attitude, knowledge or skill behavior through learning experience to achieve effective performance in an activity or range of activities. Its purpose, in the work situation, is to develop the abilities of the individual and to satisfy the current and future manpower needs of the organization" (Fox, 1994).

3.2.1.1. Training

Generally speaking, training people means partly empowering them. The empowerment idea manifests itself at all levels of societal interaction. It is found in giving voice to the disenfranchised, in allowing the weak and the marginalized to have access to the opportunity they need to forge their own destinies; in allowing each and every employee the possibility of becoming the producers of their own welfare.

There are a variety of training and development activities that are designed to increase knowledge of equal opportunity-related issues. For example, two primary diversity-training approaches are being used by various organizations: *Awareness-based Training* and *Skill-based Training*. The two approaches are interrelated and can reinforce each other, but they are different:

- *Awareness-based Training* aims at heightening awareness of diversity issues and revealing workers' unexamined assumptions and tendencies to stereotype.
- *Skill-based Training* represents a progression in intent. It goes beyond consciousness-raising, to an effort at providing workers with a set of skills to enable them to deal effectively with workplace diversity—be it in the role of manager or the role of employee.

Cox (1991) asserts that the skill-based training is enough to provide more specific information on cultural norms of different groups and how they may affect work behavior. Awareness-based training is open to criticism for its limitations. It seeks to heighten awareness, but it does not provide skills to enable participants to act more effectively. Many are finding that without skill-based training in how to deal with cultural differences, people may be at loss as to what to do with their new understanding.

Skill-based training has to have three objectives:
1. Building new diversity-interaction skills;
2. Reinforcing existing skills;
3. Inventorying skill-building methodologies.

Beyond these objectives, *"just-in-time training"* is also crucial. Just-in-time training means that training must come when the employee—that is, the learner—needs it (Watkins and Marsick, 1993). People learn best when learning is relevant and immediately available and useful.

3.2.1.2. Performance Evaluation

There is perhaps not a more important human resources system in organizations than performance evaluation. Supervisor's ratings of subordinates' performance represent critical decisions that are key influences on a variety of subsequent human resources actions and outcomes (Judge and Ferris, 1993).

Effective teams are aware of their own performance and progress toward goals (Gaddy and Wachtel, 1992). They frequently evaluate their progress and make adjustments in goals or activities (Goodman and Dean, 1982; Weingart, 1992). Teams are dynamic and evolve over time, so the long-term viability of teams requires adequate performance assessment and feedback mechanisms to allow the team to make adjustments as needed (Goodman et al., 1988).

Individual team member performance must also be monitored in order to avoid social free riding (e.g., Albanese and Van Fleet, 1985; Matsui et al., 1987). This is the tendency of people to expend less effort when working on a team as opposed to working alone. To refrain any negative effects, members must be able to differentiate their contributions from those of other members and perceive a link between their performance and team success (Levine and Moreland, 1990), that is, transparency is necessary.

Transparency is absolutely essential for any form of accountability and for understanding the factors that underlie any decision. The information should be available to everyone in a sufficiently transparent fashion so that both the costs and benefits of particular decisions and to whom such benefits accrue would be known.

Also feedback enables people to know how they affect each other, and how well they perform their tasks and meet their objectives at work. Feedback ranges from the informal comments we make about our reaction to something others do or say, to the formal performance appraisals we give each other.

Feedback rightly given and received empowers the individual by informing him/her how to behave in more effective ways, and thus gives more choice and focus to his/her efforts (Simons et al., 1993).

It makes sense to use the feedback and appraisal to improve how diversity is managed. Most managers want to be better managers of *all* their people. Given information about their performance, they are willing to learn to do things differently, accurately, and effectively.

3.2.1.3. Success Sharing

Should companies share the success with their employees? And if so, HOW? Sharing in the success of the business can be an important tool to align the employees' interests with those of the company—if employees perceive the program as fair.

The methods used to reach out to employees are broad, depending upon the size of the company involved. But the sincerity of recognition should be available to all workers. For example:

- Tennessee Valley Authority (TVA) is offering financial

incentives to all employees who contribute to the success of the agency. Successful companies such as TVA use gain sharing plans to reward their employees and to promote individual ownership of the company and its goals;
- One night a year Disneyland is open to Disney employees and their families only, with top management dressed in costumes and running the concessions and rides;
- Federal Express honors outstanding employees by christening new airplanes with the names of their children;
- WordPerfect Corporation told employees if they double sales in a year, all 600 employees would spend a week in Hawaii;
- A-P-A Transport Corporation, North Bergen, takes its 1,800 employees, their spouses or guests, on an expense-paid weekend (and has been doing so for many years);
- Warner-Lambert, Morris Plains, uses gift certificates for on-the-spot employee recognition;
- Thomas J. Lipton, Englewood Cliffs, has an Open Vending Machine Day whereby employees are allowed free access to plant cafeteria vending machines when reaching certain manufacturing goals...

Success sharing (or gain sharing) is actually one of the most rapidly growing compensation and involvement systems in U.S. industry today. It is a system of management in which an organization seeks higher levels of performance through the involvement and participation of its people. Employees share (not necessarily financially) in the success (or gain) when performance improves. The approach is a team effort in which employees are eligible for bonuses at regular intervals on an operational basis.

Success sharing also reinforces total quality management, partially because it contains common components, such as identity, involvement, and commitment. Most important to a successful success sharing endeavor is management commitment and willingness to accept change (Wilhelm, 1995).

Though most success sharing formulas are based on a ratio between direct labor costs and production value, Graham-Moore and Ross (1990) claim that, one of the objectives that has to be met to have a successful success sharing formula is the fairness of the policy established for sharing true increases in labor productivity.

3.2.2. Toward Mental Models Sharing

The idea is straightforward: adherence to a certain pattern of social relationships generates a particular way of looking at the world—that is, shared mental models; adherence to a certain worldview legitimizes a corresponding kind of visioning activity.

However, the development of shared mental models will require more lengthy and elaborate periods of interaction (Schein, 1993). Hence, the necessity of repeated interactions and social networks inside organizations. The assumption here is that if these two requirements will become common in a multicultural workplace, members will communicate better with each other, be able to foster constructive conflict, then begin to mutually understand, mutually trust and respect, and cooperate. The important goal of this process is to enable the group to reach the gradual co-creation of a shared set of meanings and a common thinking process—that is, mental models sharing.

3.2.2.1. Repeated Interactions

Interactions may emerge out of a wide variety of already established conditions, such as preexisting friendship ties or resource dependence (Galaskiewicz, 1985). These different starting points vary in the degrees to which the parties are acquainted and have had prior interactions and, thus, they vary regarding the opportunity through prior sense-making activities to come to know and understand self in relation to others. Indeed, in practice, most relationships among strangers emerge incrementally and begin with small, informal deals that initially involve little risk (Friedman, 1991). As these interactions are repeated through time, and meet basic norms of equity and efficiency—that is, satisfactory for both parties, they may be able to negotiate, make commitments, and begin to rapidly create and develop a social network.

The social networks, which are produced through an accumulation of prior interactions that were judged by the parties as being efficient and equitable, increase the likelihood that parties may be willing to make more significant and risky investments in future interactions[10]. On the contrary, repeated failures by individuals to gain confirmations of their perceptions of self in relation to others set in motion defense mechanisms and the development of a deviant identity, which will not likely lead to congruency in definition of values, purposes, or expectations.

3.2.2.2. Social Networks

Social networks consist of friends, relatives, and business associates (Sonnenberg, 1990). Networking today is no longer just a nice way to meet colleagues. It is a strategic necessity.

Sonnenberg (1990) stated that networking is a long-term strategy. Networks improve over time as their staunchest members develop them. They are important vehicles for communications in organizations (Guetzkow, 1965), thus, they can improve mutual understanding, mutual trust and respect, and cooperation. Nevertheless, they are not developed

---

[10] One may notice here that repeated interactions are just a precondition for social networks but they are still not social networks.

overnight. Successful networks change and evolve, expand and contract, and must be continually nurtured by all their members.

According to Baker (1994), the most productive attitude in a network is what psychologists call interdependence or mutual dependence. It is the recognition that you need each other. It is the recognition that people get things done through and with others. Mutual help and cooperation is therefore vitally important. An interdependent person knows that no one is an island (Baker, 1994).

Sonnenberg (1990) however argues that networking must be a give-and-take relationship because when you do too much for people without ever accepting something in return, you make recipients hesitant to ask for more and you imply that they have nothing to offer. On the contrary, help is not given on a one-for-one basis. Just because you perform a favor does not mean you should expect one in return.

With this norm of generalized reciprocity "I will do this for you now, in the expectation that somewhere down the road you'll return the favor," it is expected that:

- Networks increase the potential costs to a defector in any individual transaction since by engaging opportunism within one transaction, he puts at risk the benefits he expects to receive from all the other transactions in which he is currently engaged, as well as the benefits from future transactions.
- Networks facilitate communication and improve the flow of information about the trustworthiness of individuals.
- Networks embody past success at collaboration, which can serve as a culturally defined template for future collaboration.

The business benefits of networking can be substantial, but beyond professional life, networking can give you enormous personal pleasure and satisfaction.

3.2.2.3. Communication

Communication is often difficult between people with the same language, similar experiences, and familiar environment. It is even more so when all these factors are not shared. Many researchers (e.g., Bosche, 1993) therefore suggest the use of *Intercultural Communication*[11] whenever people belonging to different cultural groups come into contact; Hayashi (1985, 1989) proposes the concept of *Cross-cultural Interface Management* to alleviate strategic problems in culturally mixed organizations.

However, being able to slip into and out of more than one culture is a skill belonging to a limited number of the individuals. A more practical suggestion for individuals would therefore be to develop a communication network by, first, taking the step of repeated interactions.

The arrangement of communication networks or channels among members can exert a powerful influence upon team performance. Many types of networks have been investigated to determine their effects on team functioning, including wheel, Y, chain, circle, and completely connected configurations. These networks differ in ways relevant to team performance, including speed and accuracy of information transmission (e.g., decentralized channels create fewer bottlenecks). Extent information is distributed among members (e.g., members may be better informed in decentralized channels) and degree of member satisfaction with the channels—e.g., higher for decentralized (Shaw, 1981).

Even though the design of a team's communication network is not always under the control of the members, it is desirable

---

[11] *Intercultural Communication* is the ability to eliminate communication barriers such as insufficient exchange of information, semantic difficulties, different perceptions among senders and receivers, non-verbal cues that are ignored or misinterpreted, and so on.

that members have knowledge of these networks so they can implement them where and when possible.

3.2.2.4. Constructive Conflict

First of all, we must agree that without communication, there can be no question of interpersonal conflict. And thereby, without conflict, there can be no question of promoting constructive conflict!

Experts on conflict management have noted that a certain amount of interpersonal conflict is inevitable and perhaps even healthy in organizations (Northcraft and Neale, 1990). However, conflict becomes destructive when it is excessive, not well managed, or rooted in struggles for power rather than the differentiation of ideas.

The practices of constructive conflict may offer a useful alternative for managing multicultural groups, Tjosvold and Johnson (1983) declare. The constructive conflict approach builds on the idea of conflict being a key to unlock the potential group decision making. It encourages variety, openness, and challenge[12]. Group decision making can be improved by constructive conflict practices, because the knowledge and perspectives of all members are tapped and uncritical acceptance of alternatives is prevented (Schweiger et al., 1989). In the case of multicultural groups, the constructive-conflict approach could ensure that members regardless of cultural background are called upon to contribute and that the inherent diversity of such groups is valued.

Research has supported the benefits of constructive conflict to group decision making. When constructive conflict was built

---

[12] *Constructive Conflict* has not to be confused with *Competitive Conflict* which discourages both core competence sharing and exploration and can be characterized by win-lose struggles (Tjosvold and Deemer, 1980).

into the decision-making process, groups:
- Produced assumptions of greater validity and of more importance (Schweiger et al., 1986);
- Made recommendations that more often integrated the ideas and concerns of multiple parties (Tjosvold and Deemer, 1980) and that were superior in quality (Schweiger et al., 1986) than when harmony or conflict avoidance prevailed.

Furthermore, it was the presence of constructive-conflict practices, that is, searching out a variety of perspectives, openly discussing differences, and carefully critiquing assumptions and alternatives, rather than the specific format of debate, that led to higher quality decision making (Schweiger et al., 1986).

An important question remaining for those who manage multicultural groups is HOW constructive conflict can be achieved. In his study of conflict-positive organizations, Tjosvold (1991) argued that managers play a key role in setting the norms that encourage work-group members to express their opinions, doubts, uncertainties, and hunches. He advised managers to actively solicit various viewpoints, seek solutions that are responsive to several viewpoints, and reward for group successes rather than independent work. Moreover, managers or outside change agents may be required to provide training to familiarize group members with the constructive-conflict approach and to practice its implementation (Schweiger et al., 1986; Tjosvold, 1991).

3.2.2.5. Mutual Understanding

The formula for managing any relationship involves the same basic elements: mutual understanding[13] and mutual

---

[13] Multicultural understanding encompasses knowledge about how and why culturally diverse team members act the way they do, and respect for differing cultural operating style.

benefit. When there is mutual understanding, each person understands the reasons why the other acts in a particular way and accepts the other's behavior as legitimate and authentic, despite the tension or inconvenience it might cause. Each person understands the other's motives and feelings, each can take the role of the other with great empathy. When there is mutual benefit, both parties get what they need from the relationship. Each help the other. It is win-win (Baker, 1994). One may remark then that mutual understanding can be effectively achieved by fostering a social network.

3.2.2.6. Mutual Trust and Respect

Trust, the mutual confidence that no party to an exchange will exploit the other's vulnerability, is today widely regarded as a precondition for success. If trust is absent, no one will risk moving first and all will sacrifice the gains of cooperation to be safe. An area does prosper because of the cooperation which trust makes possible, though on the other hand, these same actors regard their mutual confidence as a natural fact.

Trust can also be created at will. If the reflexive view of self and society is correct, then the real problem is how trust can be built in particular circumstances through a circuitous redefinition of collective values. It is only by recognizing their mutual dependence that the actors can define their distinct interests.

In the conceptual model, it may be fair to say that individuals are trustworthy because a trustworthy reputation is useful when repeated interactions and social networks are common (that is, repeated interaction and social networks increase reputation building). A long-term orientation encourages trust because the values of short-term gains from untrustworthy actions are reduced.

In addition, an important component in effective

interpersonal relations between non-dominant and dominant cultures is the ability to express respect and positive regard for the other. When we treat people with respect, we confer status, making them feel as though they are people of importance to us. We will be expressing sincere interest in them, and they will most likely respond positively to us.

Mutual trust and respect eases collective life. The greater the level of trust and respect within a community, the greater the likelihood of cooperation.

3.2.2.7. Cooperation

Usually, people believe that cooperation emerges when people find it in their interest to do favors for each other or to help each other out. However, these favors rarely occur simultaneously. Rather, it is a case of "You do a favor for me now, and I will owe you one: I will help you on your problems next time you ask." To sustain this, the future must have a large enough shadow: those who are to cooperate must have a large enough chance of interacting with, and needing, each other again. Therefore, in great majority, the foundation of cooperation increasingly depends on the durability of the relationship (that is, repeated interactions) and networking (Simons et al., 1993).

Simons et al. (1993) argue that cross-cultural collaboration always and everywhere means changes on everybody's part. Working side by side, pursuing the same processes, and producing the same product always demands that people create common mental models, which may differ from that which they have.

3.2.2.8. Mental Models Sharing

A team or a group with a shared mental model is one where most, if not all, of the people involved think about a phenomenon or situation in a very similar manner (e.g., Cannon-Bowers et al., 1993). This seems straightforward enough.

According to Marsick (1994), mental models are not unchangeable, they are the collective creation of people. Therefore they can be changed by agreement of people. However, he emphasized, they have to be made publicly discussible and questionable.

Shared mental models are assumed to enhance the quality of teamwork skills and team effectiveness (Cannon-Bowers et al., 1990, 1993; Orasanu and Salas, 1993). Specifically, it is hypothesized that the greater the overlap or commonality among team members' mental models, the greater the likelihood that team members will predict the needs of the task and team, adapt to changing demands, and coordinate activity with one another successfully (Cannon-Bowers et al., 1993). Teams who share mental models are expected to have common expectations of the task and team, allowing them to predict the behavior and resource needs of team members more accurately (Cannon-Bowers et al., 1990).

Shared team models work by virtue of their capacity for allowing individual members to anticipate and predict the behavior of individual members and the probable behavior of the group (when there is occasion to operate as a group). This capacity, in turn, allows for the efficient and effective use of team member inputs (Klimosky and Mohammed, 1994).

My view of shared mental models therefore presumes that:
- They are an emergent characteristic of the group, which is more than just the sum of individual models (Klimosky and Mohammed, 1994).

- They represent efforts to simplify events or responsibilities in order to make them more tractable (Klimosky and Mohammed, 1994).
- They reflect organized knowledge (Klimosky and Mohammed, 1994). Usually they are in the form of a set of concepts stored and retrieved from memory in relationship to one another.
- They imply a variety of contents. While life would be simpler if we could conclude that mental models always implicate a specific domain, we feel that this is not the case. We allow therefore that the content of shared mental models might reference representation of tasks, of situations, of response patterns or of working relationships.
- They reflect internalized beliefs, assumptions, and perceptions. They are therefore really how the group members, as a collectivity, think or characterize phenomena.

Some prior writers argue that decisions can be made in the absence of a team mental model and despite differences of interpretation among individuals (e.g., Donnellon et al., 1986; Weick, 1979). Time pressure, for example, may force a group to arrive at a decision without members sharing perceptions and beliefs on the issues under consideration. It is even possible that team mental models may not emerge until after the decision phase if the team continues to interact and discuss concerns. However, team mental models could have a major influence on the implementation of a decision (providing that the team also has to implement what it has decided on). Teams that have well-developed mental models may be able to implement their decisions more quickly and with fewer problems than teams that do not have collective mental models (Klimosky and Mohammed, 1994).

One of the first large corporations to discover the potential power of mental models was Royal Dutch/Shell. It is truly multicultural, formed originally in 1907 from "a gentlemen's agreement" between Royal Dutch Petroleum and the London-based Shell Transport and Trading Company. Managing a highly decentralized company through the turbulence of the world oil business in the 1970s, Shell found that, by helping managers clarify their assumptions, uncover internal contradictions in those assumptions, and think through new strategies based on new assumptions, they gained a unique source of competitive advantage. Royal Dutch/Shell now has more than a hundred operating companies around the world led by managers from almost as many different cultures.

Developing an organization's capacity to work with mental models involves both repeated and open interactions and networks that help bring these interactions into efficiency. Because of the increasing rate of change in the environment (e.g., due to immigration/migration and technological complexity), organizations face an increasing need for learning. Consequently:

- People from different cultural backgrounds are more and more likely to work together in a similar environment (implying different languages and assumptions about reality, that is, different mental models).
- Organizations and their subunits are more and more likely to develop their own cultures (implying different languages and assumptions about reality between organizations and between subunits, that is, different mental models).

Organizational effectiveness is therefore increasingly dependent on valid communication, constructive conflict, mutual understanding, mutual trust and respect, and cooperation across culture boundaries. Integration across cultures (between individual or cultural groups and between organizations or subunits) will increasingly hinge on the ability to develop overarching common mental models.

In addition, any form of organizational learning will require the evolution of shared mental models that cut across the interacting cultures; and the evolution of new shared mental models is inhibited by current cultural rules about interaction, making them a necessary second step in learning.

3.2.3. Toward Vision Sharing

The essence of a team is shared vision. Without it, groups perform as individuals; with it, they become a powerful unit of collective learning.

Block (1987) asserts that managers empower when they create a vision of greatness. However, empowerment will not take place if executives merely create a vision, and then pass it down through successive levels of the organization to reinterpret and implement. Empowerment occurs through mutual creation of a common vision[14]. Mutual creation implies dialogue and modification of the vision up, down, and across levels. Visioning is a collective process (Watkins and Marsick, 1993) and empowerment interrupts the status quo.

It is however naive to think that co-creation of a vision is easy to achieve without the two preconditions cited above, that is, success sharing and mental models sharing. Members of diverse groups generally have problems in agreeing on their purpose and on what tasks to perform. To maximize the

---

[14] Co-creation of vision supposes that the vision would be based on employees' common needs, aspirations, and goals, disregarding their cultural backgrounds. It will enhance goal acceptance (Matsui et al., 1987; Pearson, 1987) and may increase congruence between individual and team goals (Erez, 1986; Mackie and Goethals, 1987). It may also lead to better quality goals and greater satisfaction with the process (Levine and Moreland, 1990).

effectiveness, the manager and team leader must help the group to agree on a vision that transcends their individual differences.

When people work together toward a common objective, teams inevitably hold themselves responsible, both as individuals and as a team. This sense of mutual accountability also produces the rich rewards of mutual achievement in which all members share (Katzenbach and Smith, 1993).

Senge (1990) said that purpose is similar to a direction, a general heading. Vision is a specific destination, a picture of a desired future. Purpose is abstract, vision is concrete. The organizational vision—whether it addresses the company's products, working environment, or quality of workforce—should provide a vivid picture that inspires employees and managers alike. Real visions have meaning as they are realized in particular designs, products, processes, and services (Savage, 1990).

The power to act must be directed toward something. In a learning organization, leaders help people create a collective vision toward which the entire organization can work (Watkins and Marsick, 1993). By learning to share perspectives, or mental models, teams make aligned action possible. A key task in creating the learning organization is to create alignment by placing the vision in the hands of synergistic teams. These teams need support through enhancement of their team learning effectiveness and creation of routine methods to capture and share their learning with the rest of the organization (Watkins and Marsick, 1993).

The learning organization must begin with a shared vision, Watkins and Marsick (1993) declare. Learning is directed toward that vision. Learning organizations depend on the participation of many individuals in a collective vision and on the release of the potential locked within them.

3.2.4. Toward Core Competence Development

The idea of learning organization is not new (Pedler et al., 1991) but the notion of core competence development through multicultural learning has only begun because core competence development has been identified as the hallmark of today's companies. Individuals should learn if social aggregates are to learn. Managers could involve social units in collective learning—aggregates of people who are united by the pursuit of common vision. A collective process—in which core competence is developed—should therefore take place in such a way that social units learn (Prahalad and Hamel, 1990; Marsick, 1994) and develop core competence.

The challenge is to develop mechanisms to capture, save, and share gains of learning (Ghoshal, 1987; Watkins and Marsick, 1993). However, up to now, it is not clear which mechanisms work best and what conditions prompt access and utilization for learning. What is known is that capturing and sharing the gains (of learning) depends on the existence of exchange mechanisms (Ghoshal, 1987; Marsick, 1994).

Furthermore, Ghoshal (1987) attributes critical importance to diversity of skills and learning for enhancing the firm's capacity to survive [and to develop core competence][15]:

> "... *Diversity creates the potential for learning [and developing core competence]. To exploit this potential, the organization must consider learning [and core competence development] as an explicit objective and must create mechanisms and systems for such learning [and core competence development] to take place. In the absence of*

---

[15] The terms between brackets [ ] were added by the author to show the inseparability of learning (and multicultural learning) and core competence development.

> *explicit intention and appropriate mechanisms, the learning potential [and competitive advantages] may be lost."*

Since ethnic and cultural diversities are "natural" sources of requisite variety, which is a condition for organizational learning, both managerial and individual learning would be crucial elements for developing core competence, thus, successfully managing multicultural organizations.

Here, it is argued that if the above-mentioned preconditions—success sharing, mental model sharing, vision sharing—are satisfied, an environment that fosters core competence development through multicultural learning can be *effectively* and *easily* generated.

The following steps of the learning process should take place after vision sharing (Figure 5).

1. *Core Competence Searching/Acquisition.* Logically, a learning process should begin with core competence searching/acquisition from inside and/or from outside the company; through formal (e.g., training at local specialized schools) and/or informal (e.g., friendship) channels. Normally, core competence acquisition requires time and may occur by chance and/or by careful planning. Moreover, the relevance of possible core competence is often difficult to know long in advance when it is needed.

2. *Selection and Adaptation.* Newly acquired core competence does not always fit easily with the existing organizational core competence, hence, the need to select and to adapt them. Selecting the very needed core competence when there are so many, and trying each bit for fit with the existing organizational core competence is, however, no easy task.

   Adaptiveness involves both exploitation and exploration. Exploitation refers to the improvement, refinement, routinizing, and elaboration of existing core competence and the tying of this competence with another core competence newly acquired to produce a joint product. Exploration refers to experimentation with new core competence in the hope of finding alternatives that improve on the old one. Exploitation and exploration are linked in an enduring symbiosis. Each is dependent on the other to contribute effectively to an organization's survival and prosperity (March, 1995).

Though the failure risk of an adaptive phase seems to be higher in a more culturally diverse workforce than in a less culturally one (because of the disparity in competencies in these groups), the pool of competencies in the first group has a higher potential to be richer than that of the second group.

Furthermore, since unlearning trap is negatively correlated to the pool of competencies richness, one may deduce that the risk of unlearning is lower in a more culturally diverse group.

3. *Experimentation.* At this stage, employees test newly acquired core competence by using scientific and non-scientific methods simultaneously. Usually, this activity involves "learning by mistakes" and/or "learning by doing".

In this book, these three first steps are classified as **lower-level learning** since the employees are not basically motivated by expanding horizons (Figure 5).

4. *Core Competence Development.* Core competence development is important because of its impact on individual and team practices in a learning organization. Usually, this activity involves learning from others, improving, and transferring of core competence (the joint product). Developed core competence can be a terrific asset because it comes from looking outside one's immediate environment to gain a new perspective and it is a powerful

motor for a co-creation of new core competence.

In learning organizations, people also develop core competence through informal conversations. For example, a study by Xerox Corp.'s Palo Alto Research Center showed that service technicians learned the most about repairing copiers from sharing stories with each other—not from reading manuals.

5. *Co-creation of New Competence.* At this stage, employees work together with a constant determination to improve on what has been and what should be done and/or to co-create new core competence towards the shared vision.

These two last steps are named **higher-level learning** because they are the development of the mind to think in terms of whole systems and complete processes (Figure 5).

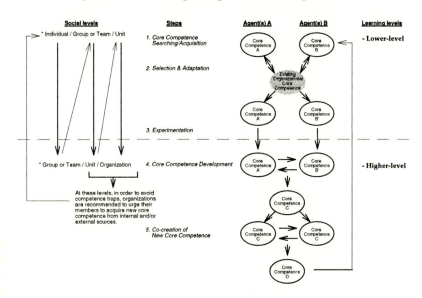

Figure 5: A dynamic model of learning process

Fiol and Lyles (1985) suggest that higher-level learning is more prevalent in firms with a diverse environmental context than from those in more homogeneous environments. Beyond the lower-level learning, which generally involves only repetition of past behaviors with few associations being formed, the higher-level learning aims to create new insight, heuristics, and a collective consciousness within the organization (Fiol and Lyles, 1985).

Levitt and March (1988) state that the higher-level learning often produces specialization and highly differentiated organization designs that promote nonroutine behavior. As Barney (1991) and other researchers noted, firm-level specialization helps introduce a causal ambiguity that makes competitive imitation of firm-specific resources difficult (Reed and DeFillipi, 1990). The specialization based on core competence is difficult to imitate and, thus, can provide the basis for a sustainable competitive advantage.

A genuine learning organization has to dedicate itself to develop the higher-level learning of its entire people, not just some at the middle and a few at the top (Teramoto et al., 1993a; 1993b). That is, for an organization to receive the full benefits of a multicultural workforce, it is essential for higher-level learning to permeate it from the bottom up.

Core competence can be transferred from one individual to another and from the team to the rest of the organization to achieve unified action on a shared vision. The establishment of mechanisms to exchange and share what teams learn is a key element in creating the learning organization (Marsick, 1994; Teramoto et al., 1994; Watkins and Marsick, 1993). That is managing cultural diversity, which itself is the essence of the sharing principle proposed in the model.

Over time, core competence may become organization-specific. These resources can, however, also act as *traps* or *rigidities*. This facet of core competence sharing can be particularly devastating for businesses that wish to compete on the basis of new products and markets. Internally developed, core competence focuses attention and momentum of activities in a certain direction thereby reducing an organization's learning and innovative capabilities. Consequently, it would be suggested that organizations could attempt to break these traps by acquiring (searching, buying) new and diverse competencies from internal and external sources (refer to the first step of the learning process) before existing competence become organization-specific. Hence, the importance of the notion of dynamic core competence.

3.2.5. Toward Co-success

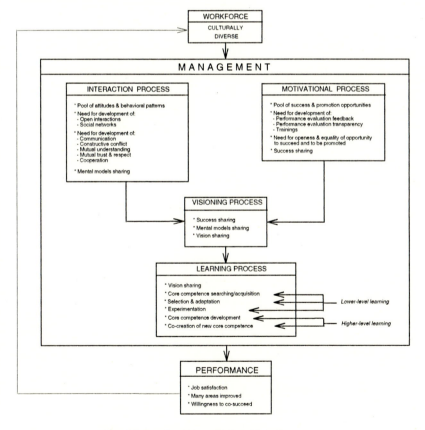

Figure 6: Conceptual model for an effective multicultural management

A long time ago, literature claimed that cultural diversity often leads to lower performance. Studies conducted over the past three decades, (e.g., Copeland, 1988; Cox et al., 1991; Esty, 1988; Mandell and Kohler-Gray, 1990; Marmer-Solomon, 1989) however, agree that, when properly managed, culturally diverse groups and organizations have performance advantages over homogeneous ones. In addition, many writers such as Adler (1991) and Kumar et al. (1991) found that the common element among high performing groups with high diversity is the integration of that diversity.

This chapter has developed and proposed a practical and realistic integration of employees' skills and abilities, attitudes and behaviors, knowledge and experiences, ways of thinking, ways of doing, and so on through **the sharing principle**—sharing successes, sharing mental models, sharing vision, and sharing competence—for effective multicultural learning and, thus, toward a real co-success (Figure 6).

3.3. Specific Hypotheses

3.3.1. Effects of Cultural Distances

Prior researchers such as Hofstede (1980, 1991) and Jaeger (1990) assert that cultural values from the environment are brought into the workplace and have a strong influence on the behavior, attitudes, and perceptions of the persons within the organization. This assertion however does not clearly reflect the real and full issues about multicultural environment within an organization unless we take the position that culture does matter if cultural distances between team and organizational members do matter. Indeed, it is rather the cultural differences or distances which bring cultural clashes within teams and organizations. Thus, the following series of hypotheses would be suggested:

> HYPOTHESIS 1a: Cultural distances between the cultural groups will affect their success sharing.
>
> HYPOTHESIS 2a: Cultural distances between the cultural groups will affect their mental models sharing.
>
> HYPOTHESIS 3a: Cultural distances between the cultural groups will affect their vision sharing.
>
> HYPOTHESIS 4a: Cultural distances between the cultural groups will affect their core competence development.

From the same perspective, since within a multicultural workplace cultural groups' members do have various cultures (creating various behavior and mental programs [Hofstede, 1980; 1984; 1990]), that regulate their perceptions of things and orientations (Simons et al., 1993), the effects of cultural distances on success sharing, mental models sharing, vision sharing, and core competence development would not be the same for all cultural groups. In other words:

> HYPOTHESIS 1b: The effect of cultural distances on success sharing will not be the same for all of the cultural groups.
>
> HYPOTHESIS 2b: The effect of cultural distances on mental models sharing will not be the same for all of the cultural groups.
>
> HYPOTHESIS 3b: The effect of cultural distances on vision sharing will not be the same for all of the cultural

groups.

HYPOTHESIS 4b: The effect of cultural distances on core competence development will not be the same for all of the cultural groups.

These hypotheses conform to the aforementioned definition of multicultural management, which considers the motivational, the interaction, the visioning, and the learning processes simultaneously.

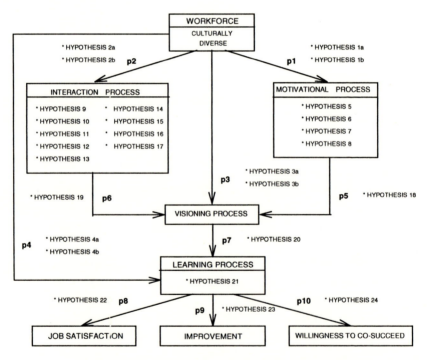

Figure 7: Relationships between the conceptual model and the hypotheses

3.3.2. Conditions for an Effective Multicultural Management

3.3.2.1. Success Sharing

The following hypothesis conforms to the assertion that training allows:
- The weak and the marginalized to have access to the opportunity they need to forge their own destinies;
- Each and every employee the possibility of becoming the producers of their own welfare.

That is, the purpose of training in the work situation is to develop the abilities of the individual and to satisfy the current and the future manpower needs of the organization (Fox, 1994). All employees from all cultural backgrounds would therefore view training as a factor leading to an open and equal opportunity to succeed and be promoted. In other words:

> HYPOTHESIS 5: All employees from all cultural backgrounds will recognize that the more training they receive, the more open and equal their opportunity to succeed and be promoted will be.

Prior researchers such as:
- Simons et al.'s (1993) assert that job performance feedback is needed to inform the individual about how to behave in more effective ways, and thus gives more choice and focus on his/her efforts;
- Levine and Moreland's (1990) state that job performance transparency is necessary to refrain any negative effects and to enable members to differentiate their contributions from those of other members.

It is therefore likely that employees from all cultural backgrounds would view job performance evaluation feedback and transparency as a healthy contribution to an open and equal opportunity to succeed and be promoted. In other words:

> HYPOTHESIS 6: All employees from all cultural backgrounds will recognize that the more job performance evaluation feedback they receive, the more open and equal their opportunities to succeed and be promoted will be.

> HYPOTHESIS 7: All employees from all cultural backgrounds will recognize that the more job performance evaluation is transparent, the more open and equal their opportunities to succeed and be promoted will be.

Van Auken (1993) says that cultures may vary but people's needs and motives are remarkably universal. All employees, for example:
- Have the need to feel productive and that they have earned their pay;
- Respond to rewards, whether tangible or psychological, offered for performance.

They would however be motivated to produce more and better outcomes if all team members would have an open and equal opportunity to participate and to succeed in a given activity. Hence, the following hypothesis:

> HYPOTHESIS 8: All employees from all cultural backgrounds will recognize that the more their opportunities to succeed and be promoted are open and equal, the more there will be success sharing.

3.3.2.2. Mental Models Sharing

According to Marsick (1994), mental models are not unchangeable. They are the collective creation of people, and hence can be changed or dissolved and/or co-created and shared by agreement of the people. Schein (1993) adds that, within a multicultural workplace, shared mental models require more lengthy and elaborate periods of interactions because of the effects of cultural distances. Repeated and open interactions and social networks would therefore be needed to bring the culturally diverse workforce's interactions into efficiency. In other words:

> HYPOTHESIS 9: All employees from all cultural backgrounds will recognize that the more repeated interactions and social networks there are, the better their communication will be.
>
> HYPOTHESIS 10: All employees from all cultural backgrounds will recognize that the more repeated interactions and social networks there are, the less conflicts there will be.
>
> HYPOTHESIS 11: All employees from all cultural backgrounds will recognize that the more repeated interactions and social networks there are, the more they will understand each other.
>
> HYPOTHESIS 12: All employees from all cultural backgrounds will recognize that the more repeated interactions and social networks there are, the more they will trust and respect each other.
>
> HYPOTHESIS 13: All employees from all cultural

backgrounds will recognize that the more repeated interactions and social networks there are, the more cooperation there will be.

If these two requirements would become common in a multicultural workplace, an environment that is suitable for mental models sharing would be easily generated. That is:

> HYPOTHESIS 14: All employees from all cultural backgrounds will recognize that the better their communication is, the more mental models sharing there will be.

> HYPOTHESIS 15: All employees from all cultural backgrounds will recognize that the more they understand each other, the more mental models sharing there will be.

> HYPOTHESIS 16: All employees from all cultural backgrounds will recognize that the more they trust and respect each other, the more mental models sharing there will be.
> HYPOTHESIS 17: All employees from all cultural backgrounds will recognize that the more they cooperate, the more mental models sharing there will be.

3.3.2.3. Vision Sharing

Multicultural management requires vision not just on the part of the strategic leaders wherever they are in the organization (James and Snell, 1994), but also among all the employees. That is why, Watkins and Marsick (1993) assert that visioning is a collective process. However, it would be naive to imagine that vision sharing is easy to achieve within a multicultural workplace without success sharing and mental models sharing. Hence, the following hypotheses:

> HYPOTHESIS 18: All employees from all cultural backgrounds will recognize that the more success sharing there is, the more vision sharing there will be.

> HYPOTHESIS 19: All employees from all cultural backgrounds will recognize that the more mental models sharing there is, the more vision sharing there will be.

3.3.2.4. Core Competence Development

The following hypothesis is based on Watkins and Marsick's (1993) statement that learning organization must begin with vision sharing and must be directed toward that vision. Furthermore, learning—a collective process in which core competence is developed—across cultural boundaries could not be created or sustained without a shared vision. In other words:

> HYPOTHESIS 20: All employees from all cultural backgrounds will recognize that the more vision sharing there is, the more core competence development there will be.

Cultural diversity is a natural source of requisite variety—which is a condition for organizational learning. However, if social aggregates are to learn, first, individuals usually must learn. In other words:

> HYPOTHESIS 21: All employees from all cultural backgrounds will recognize that their higher-level learning is directly related to their lower-level learning success.

3.3.3. Linkage Between Core Competence Development and Performance

The following hypotheses conform to the assertion that, since core competence development is and has been identified as a measure rod of higher performance in today's new reality, before multicultural workforce and multicultural companies can and keep improving, they first must develop their distinctive core competence. In other words:

> HYPOTHESIS 22: All employees from all cultural backgrounds will recognize that the more they develop their core competence, the more satisfaction they will have.

> HYPOTHESIS 23: All employees from all cultural backgrounds will recognize that the more they develop their core competence, the more improvement there will be.

> HYPOTHESIS 24: All employees from all cultural backgrounds will recognize that the more they develop their competence, the more they will be willing to co-succeed.

Chapter 4
STANDING IN THE GAP

4.1. Quantitative Study

Two kinds of questionnaires were sent to KRAOMA and STAR[16]: (1) a questionnaire for the management and (2) a questionnaire for the sample employees[17].

4.1.1. Questionnaire for the Management

4.1.1.1. Purpose and Design

In order to gain insights of Madagascarian organizations, a list of questions with an introductory letter enclosing the research plan and purposes have been sent to KRAOMA and STAR's management before the survey.

The list of questions was constructed to give insights on Madagascarian firms' reality and their strategies concerning cultural diversity.

4.1.1.2. Contents

The list consisted of 75 questions related to:
- Company's profile
- Human resource management
- Production system
- Financial situation
- Decision making
- Company's vision

---

[16] See **Chapter 5**.
[17] The sample employees consist of managers and simple employees.

- Personnel representation
- Multiculturalism

4.1.1.3. Collection of Data

Each company's management was required, in the introductory letter, to send, if possible, any potential data related to each answer of the questions before the survey, so that a relevant and appropriate questionnaire could be developed.

4.1.2. Questionnaire for the Employees

4.1.2.1. Purpose and Design

In order to gather a large body of evidence about multicultural workforce, the effects of cultural diversity on management, and the conditions for an effective multicultural management, a survey was conducted with samples of employees from the two aforementioned companies.

The questionnaire was designed to:
- Measure the workforce's cultural diversity;
- Evaluate the effects of cultural distances on management;
- Assess the firms' multicultural management—that is, multicultural learning and core competence development;
- Appraise the relationships between cultural diversity, management, and performance.

In order to avoid any misunderstanding and to gather better data, the questionnaire was carefully constructed to ask the respondent's:
1. Personal data
2. Occupational and motivational conditions
3. Interactions with other employees
4. Skills, experiences, and know-how nurturing and

development
5. Concern in the company's long-term goal or vision
6. Viewpoint on the organizational performance
7. Career history
8. Values

4.1.2.2. Contents

Section 1: Personal Data Inventory

Section 1 of the questionnaire was a standard personal inventory that asked the respondent to detail information on age, ethnic group, sex, marital status, educational level, present occupational category and position, and language ability.

Section 2: Occupational and Motivational Conditions

This measure concerned with the respondent's contract, job, type of pay, personal annual gross income, most preferred incentives, training, job performance evaluation, interest in the company's annual result, and motivation.

Section 3: Interactions with Other Employees

This measure was performed in three ways:
1. The respondent's preferred leadership style was evaluated with a scale from 1 (Never) to 5 (Always).
2. His/her interactions, similarities, and communications with other employees was assessed with a scale from 1 (Strongly disagree) to 5 (Strongly agree).

Ten points considered being the most common sources of conflicts between employees were presented. Differences in gender, age, educational level, occupational level, religion, political conviction, nationality, regional origin (ethnic group), social class, and section/service/department. The respondent was asked to check all points, which were probable sources of friction with co-workers at the workplace. The scale used was from 1 (Never) to 5 (Always).

Section 4: Skills, Experiences, and Know-how Nurturing and Development

This measure was performed by asking the respondent:
1. Whether he/she is learning something in his/her job or not. The scale used was from 1 (Nothing) to 5 (Many things).
2. How does he/she usually learn. The evaluation was based on a scale from 0 (Not applicable) to 5 (Through formal discussions with team members and supervisors).

Section 5: Concern in the Company's Vision

The measurement was performed in two ways:
1. By asking the respondent whether he/she knows the vision of the company or not. The scale used was from 1 (I have never heard) to 5 (I know and fully understand).
2. By evaluating the respondent's opinion and concern about the vision with a scale from 0 (Not applicable) to 5 (I like it and I am doing my best for its achievement).

Section 6: Viewpoint on the Organizational Performance

This section measured:
1. How well the respondent does like his/her job. The scale used was from 1 (Dislike) to 5 (Very much).
2. The respondent's job satisfaction with a scale from 1 (Not satisfied) to 5 (Very satisfied).
3. The areas that need improvement. The scale used was from 1 (Need a big improvement) to 5 (Already perfect).

4. The respondent's willingness to share and co-succeed with the other employees. The evaluation was based on a scale from 1 (Strongly disagree) to 5 (Strongly agree).

Section 7: Career History

This measure asked standard questions about the respondent's career history.

Section 8: Values

20 points considered being the most common values were presented:

1. Group/team harmony	11. Competition
2. Group/team success	12. Seniority
3. Group/team consensus	13. Privacy
4. Cooperation	14. Social recognition
5. Openness to others	15. Freedom
6. Equality	16. Status and prestige
7. Family security	17. Self-reliance
8. Relationships	18. Sense of achievement
9. Loyalty	19. Power and authority
10. Communication	20. Material possessions

In this section, the respondent was asked to check his/her five first important values.

4.1.2.3. Sources of Data

The survey was designed to measure the workforce's cultural diversity, evaluate the effects of cultural distances on management, assess the firms' multicultural management—that is, multicultural learning and core competence development, and appraise the relationships between cultural diversity, management, and performance, using the sample of KRAOMA and STAR's employees.

The sampled employees were men and women with varying cultural backgrounds, occupational levels, with differing levels of education, and with diverse social backgrounds. In order to qualify for participation in the study, each subject had to be an employee of one of the two aforementioned companies when the survey was conducted.

4.1.2.4. Collection of Data

For each company, 150 copies of the questionnaire, each with a cover letter explaining the purposes of the study, were mailed to the management, who collected the data after the investigation. As some of the questions touched on sensitive issues, it was important to ensure the employees' anonymity:
1. The cover letter asked each employee:
    A) Not to write his/her name on the copy of questionnaire;
    B) To put his/her copy of questionnaire in the envelop that has been sent from Japan and to seal the envelop before returning it back to the management;
    C) To fill out the questionnaire on the spot so that all of the sample employees would return their answers at the same time.
2. In fact, after the filled copies of questionnaire had been returned, there was no way to link specific responses with specific respondents.

The questions were asked in Malagasy and in French and were worded using terminology in common use in the organizations.

4.2. Case Study

4.2.1. Purpose and Design of the Interview

In order to have insights of multicultural organizations, interviews were conducted with employees of ERICSSON TOSHIBA[18].

The interviews were constructed to give insights on the strategies being used or which can be used in organizations, the improvements advanced by the cultural diversity in management, and the approach that would promote and develop these benefits.

4.2.2. Contents of the Interview

The interviews consisted of 40 open-ended questions related to the interviewees' personal data, the company's historical backgrounds, the multicultural management at ERICSSON TOSHIBA, and the firm's uniqueness.

4.2.3. Process of the Interview

The process of the interviews involved the following steps:
- **Step1:**
  - ✓ Preparation of the aforementioned list of questions;
  - ✓ Mailing of the list of questions with an introductory letter enclosing the research plan and purposes to the interviewees before the appointments;
- **Step2:**
  - ✓ Recording and notes during the interviews;
  - ✓ Spontaneous additional questions;
  - ✓ Gathering of data relating to some of the questions;

---

[18] See **Chapter 6**.

- **Step3:**
    - ✓ Summary of each interviewee's answers;
    - ✓ Compilation of summarized answers;
    - ✓ Identification of keypoints;
    - ✓ Asking additional information by telephone, fax, and e-mail;
    - ✓ Further analysis of the identified keypoints.

The questions were asked in Japanese if the interviewee was Japanese, in English if otherwise.

Chapter 5
QUANTITATIVE ANALYSIS: THE CASES OF KRAOMA & STAR

5.1. Presentation of Madagascar

5.1.1. Geographical Situation

MADAGASCAR is an island in the Indian Ocean, separated from the east cost of Africa by the Mozambique Channel. Its length and average breadth are about 1600 km and 570 km respectively. Madagascar's coast line is around 5,000 km long and the whole territory covers an area of 587,051 sq. km, divided into six provinces (Table 1):

Table 1: The six provinces of Madagascar
(Source: 1994 World Factbook - Madagascar (U.S. CIA))

Provinces	Areas (sq. km)	Areas (%)	Rank
Antananarivo	58,283	9.93	5
Antsiranana	43,056	7.33	6
Fianarantsoa	102,373	17.44	3
Mahajanga	150,023	25.56	2
Toamasina	71,911	12.25	4
Toliary	161,405	27.49	1
TOTAL	587,051	100.00	

5.1.2. Population and Cultures

Madagascar is anthropologically rich. Where else can one find a population with such *diverse origins,* all mixed together on one large island?
● **Indonesia:** according to researchers, the westward

migration began about two thousand years ago from the eastern side of the Indian Ocean. Successive waves of Indonesian migrants followed the sea currents in their canoes and settled on the almost empty island of Madagascar.
- **India:** according to Diogo Lopes de Sequiera, Goudjerat Indians came to Tolagnaro (south of Madagascar) around 1300. Then, Banians, Khodias, and Malabar Indians immigrated from the northwest of the island during the 13rd and 14th centuries. However, their number increased enormously from 1872 (Grandidier and Grandidier, 1951).
- **Arabia:** according to previous researchers, Azd of Oman and Karmathes Arabs began to settle on the north-east of Madagascar from the 11th century, and on the south of the island from the 16th century (Grandidier and Grandidier, 1951).
- **Europe:** according to researchers, they were Portuguese navigators, pirates from the Bermudes Islands and Boston, and Dutch (Grandidier and Grandidier, 1951).
- **Africa:** according to researchers, the migration of African people did not occur during an earlier period. The crossing from the African southeast coast to Comoros Islands and Madagascar is difficult because of the sea currents, which flow toward the continent (it is easy from the opposite direction), and Africans were not at all good mariners and did not have ocean-worthy vessels. Therefore, maybe Arab slave-dealers brought almost all of those who came to the island as slaves during the 19th century. The slave trade was at least the principal commerce of Arabs in Madagascar (Grandidier and Grandidier, 1951).

In what other country can one find so many peoples who, despite their diverse origins, and the diversity of ecology and lifestyles, all share the same language, the **"MALAGASY"**[19]?

The cultures and population of Madagascar, like that of most other places, have diverse roots. Because of this mixture of cultures and peoples, important linguistic, cultural, and physical variations occur in Madagascar. Indian, Arabic, Indonesian, European and African institutions have been thoroughly blended into a unique and varied island culture. This blend of cultures is both a curse and a blessing to anthropological studies of Madagascar.

According to the latest estimates (1994), the total population was 13,427,758 of which half resides in Antananarivo and Fianarantsoa provinces (Table 2).

Table 2: Madagascar's population by province
(Source: 1994 World Factbook - Madagascar (U.S. CIA))

Provinces	Inhabitants 1994	Inhabitants (%)	Rank	Inhabitants (per sq. km)	Rank
Antananarivo	4,369,393	32.54	1	74.94	1
Antsiranana	1,016,481	7.57	6	23.61	4
Fianarantsoa	2,952,764	21.99	2	28.84	2
Mahajanga	1,376,345	10.25	5	9.17	6
Toamasina	1,980,594	14.75	3	27.54	3
Toliary	1,732,181	12.90	4	10.73	5
TOTAL	**13,427,758**	**100.00**			

Its young population also characterizes Madagascar. About 50% of the total population is less than 18 years old, 73% of the inhabitants are less than 30 years old, and around 90% are less than 50 years old.

Since full independence from France in 1960, the population has steadily increased due to improved social conditions, reduced mortality and a rise in the number of women of childbearing age. The urban population has particularly increased, rising from 11% of the total population in 1960 to

---

[19] The MALAGASY language is—certain Bantu, Arabic, English, and French contributions notwithstanding—unquestionably a member of the Malayo-Polynesian language group.

over 20% now.

The working population constitutes around 55% of the total, and is divided among sectors as follow[20]:
- Primary Sector: 87%
- Secondary Sector: 4%
- Tertiary Sector: 9%

The people of Madagascar are composed of **18 ethnic groups** and many other clans. All provinces are multiethnic/multicultural and each province's boarders are just virtual. In other words, all of the ethnic groups cited below could be found in all the provinces though they are basically in majority in their own provinces. Prior researchers have categorized the different ethnic groups in Madagascar into three main groups, according to their geographical situation[21], activities, work ethics, and cultures mainly (Covell, 1987):
1. The **Coastal group**
2. The **Highland group**
3. The **Merina group**

Prior studies found that, since the kingdom era, the Merina group holds both the power (educational, social, economic, and political) and the dominant culture.

Globally, the three groups' sites could be schematized as follow (Figure 8).

---

[20] Source: *"Investing in Madagascar,"* a brochure printed by the Ministry of Industry, Energy, and Mining, Antananarivo, Madagascar.

[21] Though, in fact, the Merina are also highlanders.

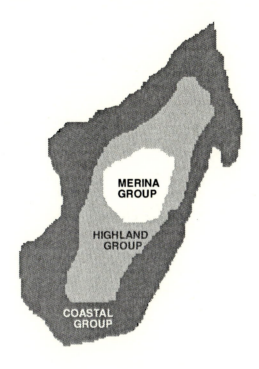

Figure 8: The cultural groups' schematized sites

From now on, the terms:
- *Cultural groups* will be used to name the three aforementioned groups;
- *Coastaler(s), Highlander(s),* and *Merina* will be used to name each of the aforementioned cultural group's members respectively.

5.1.3. Historical Background

5.1.3.1. Kingdoms Era

The ethnic groups of Madagascar were grouped to form realms in the east (Betsimisaraka), the west (Sakalava), and the south (Betsileo). In the center, the Merina built the fortified town of Antananarivo. The Merina was ruled by Andrianampoinimerina (1787-1810), then by his son Radama I (1810-1828), to whom the British conferred the title "King of Madagascar" (1817) and with whom they cooperated with in modernizing the country (Valette, 1979).

In the early years of his rule, Radama I's most pressing task was to consolidate the achievement of his father—that is, *to unify* the country. Populations outside Imerina (the Merina territory) that had been partly subject to Merina authority—that is, the Coastalers and the Highlanders—sought to exploit the change in monarchs by way of rebellions. And the incoming ruler of Imerina had to mount a number of military campaigns against them which resulted in Merina hostility (Valette, 1979).

After his death, his wife, Ranavalona I (1828-1861) closed the schools and expelled Europeans. After the reign of Radama II (1861-1863), power was transferred to Prime Minister Rainilaiarivony (1865-1895), who married successively the Queens Rasoherina, Ranavalona II, and Ranavalona III. To avoid the European seizure of the country, in 1869, he converted to Protestantism along with a significant portion of the population (Belrose-Huyghues, 1979).

5.1.3.2. Colonization

Nevertheless, by the treaty of 1885, France forcibly made the island its protectorate. Great Britain recognized this in 1890. A French expedition disembarked at Mahajanga, and with the help of mainly the angered Coastalers, they reached Antananarivo in 1895, in spite of heavy losses (6,000 men). After the capitulation of Antananarivo, the island became a French colony in 1896. General Gallieni, governor from 1896 to 1905, pacified Antananarivo and exiled Queen Ranavalona III. The colonial regime (1896-1946) overthrew the Merina oligarchic authority by restoring local chiefs and replacing Merina governors with French and Coastal governors. General Gallieni established secular education, a medical infrastructure, and presided over the island's economic development (Valette, 1979).

With the passage of time, however, Madagascar underwent a major colonial revolt in March 29, 1947. As the revolt showed without fail, nationalist resentment had real vigor. As the state of alert came to an end, it was the colonial administration's aim to regain the favor of public opinion by improving the economic and social outlays. And, more than ever, its tactic was to exploit the older rivalries between the Merina and the Coastalers—deemed to have been loyal to France (Paillard, 1979). Indeed, though the Merina and the other highlanders wanted an immediate independence, the Coastalers were against it because they were not ready at the time—they did not have enough of élites (*Courrier de Madagascar*, special number, October 12, 1968).

The Coastalers were also playing for time so that non-Merina élites would increase in numbers, improve their training, and confront at a future point in time the Merina élites on the basis of equality (Paillard, 1979).

5.1.3.3. Independence

The island became a French overseas department (1946-1958), and then an autonomous republic (1958-1960). Full independence was achieved in 1960 and France appointed Philbert Tsiranana—a Coastaler—to govern the country.

With the governmental ideology named "coastal cause" (which main purpose was to grant advantages to the Coastalers on the basis of power [educational, economic, politic, social] equality), President Tsiranana (1958-1972) maintained the apparent stability of the country. But from 1967, the opposition attacked the advantages granted to Coastal ethnic groups at the expense of the Merina. After student and worker strikes in 1972, Tsiranana transferred power to General Ramanantsoa—a Merina—and withdrew.

In 1973, negotiations were opened in Paris and new Franco-Malagasy cooperation agreements were concluded. After many of political infighting years, General Ramanantsoa transferred power to Colonel Ratsimandrava—a Merina, his Home Minister, who was then murdered while reorganizing the economy and trying to unite the country.

Frigate captain Ratsiraka—a Coastaler, who took power in the wake of the assassination, was then made President of the Supreme Council of the Revolution. The Democratic Republic of Madagascar was founded on December 31, 1975, and Ratsiraka became its president. The governmental ideology was then changed into "ethnic mixture". The economy of Madagascar however was still chronically sick and this very particular state construct was equally animated by a prolongation of the Coastal-Merina disputes, an aspect which gives the state its harshness (Paillard, 1979).

After 17 years of "Democratic Socialism," on March 9, 1993, the third republic was born following the passing of a referendum approving the new constitution and the election of Albert Zafy, a professor of surgery and the reformist leader of an opposition coalition. Zafy took over but Madagascar's dreams of a new future quickly evaporated because of infighting between the new politicians in charge, red tape, decline in world demand for coffee, and an inconsistent commitment of the government to economic growth. Moreover, public disenchantment with Zafy, who was impeach by parliament in July 1997 for repeated violations of the new constitution, was enough to earn Ratsiraka another term since February 1998.

Though the democratic choice of Madagascar opens the way to a rational and attractive liberalization whose rules will benefit from equity and transparency, in the long run, such a development would not materialize without creating a willingness-to-share environment among the different ethnic groups.

5.1.4. Madagascarian Organizations

The Madagascarian organizations are just the island's microcosms:
- Almost all-Madagascarian organizations are multiethnic and multicultural. And as it has been mentioned by Jaeger (1990), employees do not leave their cultures at the companies' doors when they come to work.
- Outside as well as inside the organizations, the cultural dominance and the economic power are basically hold by the Merina.
- Because of the above-mentioned governmental ideologies, the Madagascarian companies, mainly the national ones suffered mismanagement and were chronically sick. Indeed:
  - Recruitment and managerial positions were rather group ethnic-based than competence-based;
  - Almost all organizations do not practically have any strategy for managing multiethnic/multicultural workforce, which is yet the norm in the island.

5.2. Presentation of the Companies

5.2.1. Kraomita Malagasy (KRAOMA)

5.2.1.1. Historical Background

- **1969:** the chromite exploitation at Andriamena-Madagascar began in May and the first exportation was done in July. At that time, the company was a private company and its name

was "COmpanie MINière d'Andriamena" (COMINA).
- **1976:** nationalization of the company. Its name was then changed to "KRAOmita MAlagasy" (KRAOMA).
- **1981:** KRAOMA's statute was changed into a socialist company.
- **1992:** KRAOMA became a limited liability company.
- Since the beginning, the company's main activities are to extract, to treat, to exploit, and to commercialize the mineral of chrome (chromite).
- The capital is 1,000,000 US dollars (100% Malagasy government).
- Simultaneously with the quarry of Andriamena, KRAOMA also exploited the chromite stratums:
  - ✓ at Bemanevika from 1968 to 1973
  - ✓ at North Befandriana from 1975 to 1984

According to researchers' forecasts, the chromite reserve at Andriamena allows KRAOMA to pursue its business for at least 20 more years.

5.2.1.2. Organization Chart

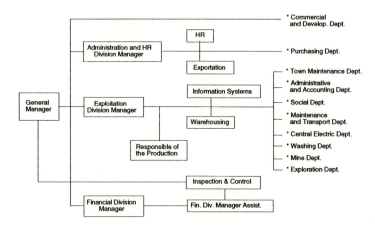

Figure 9: KRAOMA's organization chart

5.2.1.3. Evolution of the Company's Management

Evolution. The evolution was related to the different changes of the company's statute:
- National company: board of directors
- Socialist company: management committee (which includes workers)

Causes of the Evolution. Political systems changes are the main causes of the evolution.

Difficulties Encountered and Solutions.
- *Difficulties:* adaptation to the different statutes, mainly to that of socialist company. Indeed, a particular charter administers a socialist firm.
- *Solutions:* education, training, and information sharing at all organizational levels.

Changes Brought by these Steps.
- Malagasy-zation of the human resources;
- Increase of employees' participation in the management (dictated by the application of the socialist companies' charter).

5.1.2.4. Human Resource Management

Personnel Data.

Table 3: KRAOMA's personnel data from 1990 to 1995

	1990	1991	1992	1993	1994	1995
Male	399	404	411	418	404	394
Female	18	19	19	19	20	20
Total	417	423	430	437	424	414

Recruitment.
- KRAOMA does not have a fixed pre-established program of employee recruitment. The company rather practices the occasional recruitment policy.
- KRAOMA selects the employees needed through:
  - ➢ Examination of the punctual job requests;
  - ➢ Announcements in the newspapers;
  - ➢ School and/or university contacts and visits.
- In order to minimize selection subjectivity, the decision is to be made by a recruitment commission, which involves the personnel delegation.
- Potential candidates are selected without any ethnic consideration.

Training.
- The employees' training is based on the OJT system. Nevertheless, some of the employees are also sent to special courses training in local or foreign specialized organizations.
- The selection of the beneficiaries are made:
  - ➢ When the need occurs. But there is no test and/or exam;
  - ➢ By the concerned department manager and the administrative and human resource division manager;
  - ➢ Without the participation of the personnel delegation.
- Generally, in order to promote knowledge, experience, and core competence sharing within teams, daily briefing, weekly meeting, and comradeship are urged.
- KRAOMA does not educate its employees about cultural diversity because it may hurt employees' susceptibility.
- Usually, KRAOMA urges its employees to work and to succeed in teams by allowing bonuses based upon team production.

Job Performance Evaluation.
- The job performance evaluation is systematically undertook every year by the hierarchical superiors.
- The evaluation is made according to:
  - The *Output*: delay, quality, and quantity
  - The *Comportment*: esprit d'équipe, assiduity...
- KRAOMA does not have an effective method for ensuring the evaluation against subjectivity.
- The employees know and understand the evaluation process and they can receive feedback of their performance if they ask for it.

Promotion.
- There are 2 kinds of promotion at KRAOMA:
  1. Promotion to an upper echelon in a given category: systematic and based on the seniority.
  2. Promotion to an upper category, that is, changes of position in the hierarchy. If the employee passes the test to get the upper position and if the recruitment commission proposes him/her, then the general manager will make the final decision.
- Usually, the newly promoted employee is only trained for his/her new position when the need occurs, that is, the training is not systematic.
- All employees can compete for a vacant upper position, if they fulfill the required conditions for this position.

Employees' Interactions.
- KRAOMA develops mutual understanding, mutual trust and respect, and cooperation between the headquarters and the exploitation-yard and the departments and the divisions, between the management, and between employees and management by:
  1. Announcing the goals, the annual results, and their

conditions;
2. Organizing an annual general meeting.
- Beyond the job, management and workmen participate together in some activities such as re-afforestation, parties, picnics, and sport festivals...
- The company also promotes formal and informal relationships within the firm by projecting films, by organizing conferences...

Production.
- The company organizes teamworks according to the organization chart. All teams are fixed and multicultural.
- KRAOMA's strategy to make each and all teams harmonized and effective is to allow bonuses per team.

Figure 10 shows the annual gross sales and operating profits from 1985 to 1994.

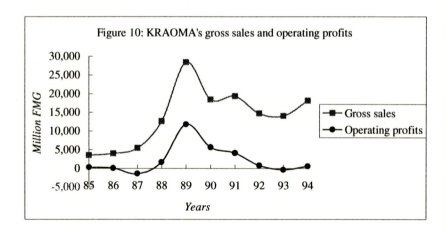

Decision-Making.
- The company's management rank is multicultural. Therefore, to make the decision-making and problem

solving effective, the company always organizes very formal meetings.
- The exploitation-yard director is allowed to make decisions on the yard's occupational and financial matters.

Company's Vision.
- The company's vision is *productivity and profitability*. This vision is displayed throughout the company.
- The company thinks that the employees share this vision because they do work hard to reach the objective according to the budget.
- KRAOMA believes that training and amelioration of the occupational conditions can lead the employees to share the company's vision.

Personnel Representation.
- Generally speaking, the company's employees are represented both by the personnel delegation and the labor unions[22].
    - ✓ Number of labor unions: 5
    - ✓ Percentage of affiliated employees: 45%
    - ✓ Non-affiliated employees are represented by the personnel delegation
- Both the members of the labor unions and the personnel delegation are multicultural. However, all the cultural groups are not represented in the personnel delegation.
- The company agrees that these groups effectively represent the employees.

Multiculturalism.
- The difficulties and problems of KRAOMA's multicultural workforce management are related to the respect of each

---

[22] Basically, the personnel delegation members are sprung from the labor unions.

employee's cultural values. That is, difficulties and problems arise because each employee's cultural values are not respected. Hence, the solution would be confined to the respect of these cultural values.
- KRAOMA hopes to see:
    - ✓ Workforce cohesiveness to attain a good result
    - ✓ Cultural exchanges among the different cultural groups
- KRAOMA does think that the keystone and keypoints for an effective multicultural management would be:
    1. Knowledge sharing involving cultural exchanges
    2. Mutual understanding and mutual respect

5.2.2. Star-MADAGASCAR (STAR)

5.2.2.1. Historical Background

- **1947:** Rochefortaise Corporation created the brewery in Antsirabe.
- **1953:** A group of independent investors got Coca-Cola's license and created STAR with Rochefortaise. At that time:
    - ✓ The firm produced and commercialized Coca-Cola's products and soda;
    - ✓ The firm's capital was FMG 30,000,000.
- **1957:** N.V. Biscorouweris "De Drie Hoefijzers" of Breda—BREDA—(Holland) joined STAR and, together, they produced the well-known "Three Horses Beer."
- **1960:** Important development and expansion of STAR's commercial agencies throughout the island. The capital attained FMG 150,000,000.
- **1966:** The Malagasy government bought 11.7% of the shares.
- **1970:** STAR bought back the actions held by BREDA.
- **1972:** STAR bought two companies—MELVINO S.A.

(wine treatment and trade) and SEMA (exploitation and distribution of mineral water).

- **1973:** STAR took over two production units of a competitor—Brasserie de Madagascar and Compagnie Générale d'Embouteillage.
- **1974:** STAR created a filial company named NY VIFOTSY (in Toliary) to produce metallic capsules for the parent company and other local bottling companies.
- **1975:** The Malagasy government increased its part in the capital to 35.39% and the capital reached FMG 1.200.000.000.
- **1976:** STAR created MALTO S.A. to study and to prepare the implementation of a malt-house in Madagascar.
- **1977:**
  1. STAR created a training center for its commercial personnel and managers.
  2. STAR let the Malagasy government have the majority of the company's capital and just hold 25% of the actions.
- **1978:** STAR created a computing related business company named KAJY MIRINDRA.
- **1982:** STAR had a deficit and this continued until 1985.
- **1986:**
  - ✓ STAR launched a new brand of beer called BEEK' BRAU.
  - ✓ The company's capital attained FMG 5.047.200.000.
- **1988:** STAR's treasury difficulty persisted because of the inflation. The capital was raised to FMG 6.548.275.000.
- **1989:**
  - ✓ The shareholders' extraordinary meeting decided to bring the company's capital to FMG 10.090.850.000.
  - ✓ The government sold its part in the capital to

Beaumont Industries S.A. who became the major shareholder.
- **1993:** The company's capital attained FMG 16.500.000.000.
- **1994:** The capital reached FMG 21.450.000.000.

5.2.2.2. Organizational Chart

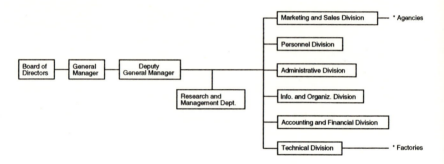

Figure 11: STAR's organization chart

STAR's main activities are to make and commercialize gasified and non-gasified beverages, alcoholic and non-alcoholic beverages.

Actually, STAR's economic environment is changing due to:
1. The economic liberalization:
   A) Appearance of new competitors;
   B) Arrival of imported competitor products;
   C) The government encourages investments and entrepreneurship.
2. The price liberalization: there is no preliminary price homology.

5.2.2.3. Evolution of the Company's Management

Like that of KRAOMA, the evolution of the management was mainly related to the different changes of the company's statute due to political changes. The difficulties were highly correlated with the adaptation of the different statutes so that the employees' education and training were found to be the most proper.

Actually, STAR became again a limited liability company so that it can now decide its financial, commercial, and investment strategies by itself.

5.2.2.4. Human Resource Management

Personnel Data.

Table 4: STAR's personnel data from 1991 to 1995

	1991	*1992*	*1993*	*1994*	*1995*
Male	1,344	1,249	1,297	1,292	1,248
Female	127	118	110	110	121
Total	**1,471**	**1,367**	**1,407**	**1,402**	**1,369**

Recruitment.
- STAR does not have a fixed pre-established program of employee recruitment. The company rather practices the occasional recruitment policy.
- STAR selects the employees needed through:
    ➢ Announcements in the newspapers;
    ➢ School and/or university contacts and visits.
- STAR has no obligation to recruit employees from all the regions.
- Generally, the personnel delegation and the labor unions do not participate in the final decision making of recruitment.

Training.
- The employees' training are based on the OJT system.
- The selection of the beneficiaries are based upon their

competencies and needs, so that after the training, they are required to improve their performance.
- Generally, in order to promote knowledge, experience, and core competence sharing within teams STAR uses the job rotation system.
- STAR educates its employees about cultural diversity:
  ➢ Through the library inside the company (books, reviews, video tapes...);
  ➢ By organizing conference debates. Sometimes, the company invites guest speakers specialized in the field of diversity.

Indeed, since STAR has a lot of agencies throughout the country and since the job rotation system is commonly used in the company, such education is crucial to run the business.
- Usually, STAR urges its employees to work and to succeed in teams by organizing regular meetings and extra-professional recreations.

Job Performance Evaluation.
- The job performance evaluation does exist but it is actually neither systematic nor periodic.
- Nevertheless, the employees know and understand the evaluation process, which allows them to defend themselves.
- Practically, the result of the job performance evaluation is communicated to the concerned employees.
- At STAR, cultural diversity does not influence the job performance evaluation.

Promotion.
- The promotion at STAR is not systematic. Only those who are competent, methodical, and assiduous could be proposed for a promotion.
- If the candidate is an executive, the General Manager

makes the final decision, otherwise, the final decision is made by the concerned department manager. The personnel delegation and the labor unions do not participate in the decision making.
- Usually, a promotion is not systematically followed or preceded by training.
- To provide its employees with an open and equal opportunity to succeed and to be promoted, STAR offers them training, job performance evaluation, and various bonuses.
- Cultural diversity does not affect the promotion at STAR.

Employees' Interactions.
- Conflicts between employees and/or agencies and/or management are very rare at STAR. Nevertheless, conflicts between recruits and senior employees sometimes occur within the different departments. The recruits have therefore sometimes integration difficulties and feel rejected.
- STAR develops mutual understanding, mutual trust and respect, and cooperation by encouraging the communication between the organizational members through different events, dance parties, exhibitions...

Production.
- Practically, all teams at STAR are fixed and multicultural because, by experience, the management found that multicultural teams are more efficient than culturally homogeneous teams.
- STAR's strategy to make each and all teams harmonized and effective is to encourage the members to communicate and to exchange their various viewpoints.

Figure 12 shows the annual gross sales and operating profits from 1988 to 1995.

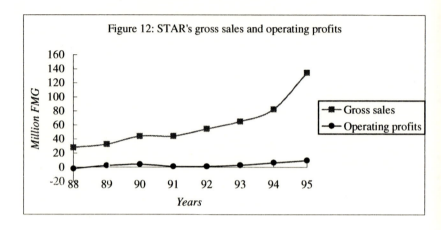

Figure 12: STAR's gross sales and operating profits

Decision-Making.
- The company's management rank is multicultural. Therefore, to make the decision-making and problem solving effective, the company always practices group decision-making and group problem solving.
- The agencies have certain autonomy in recruiting simple employees.

Company's Vision.
- The company's vision is displayed throughout the company.
- The vision is usually explained during the training.
- The company thinks that the employees share this vision.

Personnel Representation.
- Actually, there are three labor unions at STAR and 20% of the employees are affiliated with them. Non-affiliated employees are represented by the personnel delegation. That is, practically, all the company's employees are represented by the personnel delegation.

- The company agrees that the personnel delegation effectively represents the employees.

5.3. KRAOMA

5.3.1. Responses to Questionnaires

An initial request of the 150 employees in the sample yielded 110 responses (73.33%). However, 8 employees did not answer the key-questions and/or did not answer them correctly. Therefore, those 8 sets of responses were eliminated from the database. That left a sample of 102 responses to be analyzed.

5.3.2. The Sampled Employees

The sample for this study consists of 24 employees from the Coastal group (23.53%), 46 employees from the Highland group (45.01%), and 32 employees from the Merina group (31.37%). The representativeness of this sample was not evaluated since almost all of the companies in Madagascar do not have and do not disclose their personnel data by ethnic group. Therefore, as one can guess, this fact itself hints and reflects Madagascarian companies' naiveté and/or unawareness and/or sensitiveness about cultural diversity, and thereby, the inexistence of multicultural management at KRAOMA[23].

The sample is dominated by men (84 men against 18 women) and their average age is between 30 to 49 years old (Table 5). This is consistent with the firm's masculine activities, which are to extract, to treat, and to exploit the chromite.

---

[23] By formality, Madagascarian companies smooth over the cultural diversity issues yet, as we will see later on, the result of the data analysis clearly shows that the Coastalers, the Highlanders, and the Merina have various values, needs... and it does influence the company's management and performance.

Most of the sampled employees (Table 5):
- Have permanent contracts;
- Are performing manual and intellectual jobs;
- Have been paid a fixed monthly salary.

Table 5: Personal data of KRAOMA's sampled employees

Variable	Mean	Std Dev	Levels
Age	3.51	0.78	5
Contract	1.95	0.22	2
Job Nature	2.74	0.51	3
Type of Pay	2.77	0.42	6
Prior Firms	0.75	1.03	6
Years spent at KRAOMA	3.75	1.55	6
Overseas	0.04	0.28	6

According to Table 5, on average, the sampled employees had already worked for another company before coming to KRAOMA, where they have been working for about 6 to 15 years. Nevertheless, almost all of these employees did not have any overseas appointment opportunity.

5.3.3. Measurement of Cultural Diversity

First of all:
- The correlation coefficients obtained from the CORR procedure indicate that each cultural group members' answers to the questionnaire are significantly different from those of other cultural groups (Table 6);
- On average, the sampled employees are convinced that their team and organizational members do not have similar ethnic and cultural backgrounds, attitude and behavior patterns, way of thinking, and way of doing (Table 7).

Table 6: Correlations between each cultural group members' answers to the survey (KRAOMA)

	Coastalers	Highlanders	Merina
Coastalers	1.00000	-0.37505***	-0.61279***
Highlanders		1.00000	-0.50274***
Merina			1.00000

SPEARMAN correlation coefficients;   ***p<0.01

Table 7: Similarities of KRAOMA's sampled employees

Variable	Mean	Std Dev
Ethnic and/or cultural backgrounds	2.09	0.99
Promotion/Success Opportunity	2.76	1.12
Attitude and behavior patterns	2.08	0.84
Values and needs	3.12	0.96
Skills	2.14	0.86
Job Experiences	2.45	1.06
Way of thinking and doing	2.44	0.89

Level = 1 (lowest)   Very different
Level = 5 (highest)   Very similar

Power Distance. Considering the chosen indicators of Power Distance Index (PDI) in Appendix (Table A1), the statistic output from the ANOVA procedure shows that (Table 8):
1. At the 0.01 significance level, the Merina's average PDI is significantly different from that of the Coastalers.
2. At the 0.10 significance level, the Merina's average PDI is also significantly different from that of the Highlanders.

Table 8: The output of ANOVA Procedure: differences in PDI (KRAOMA)

DUNCAN's multiple range test for variable: "Power Distance Index"

Alpha = 0.01   DF = 99   MSE = 0.945315
Means with the same letter are not significantly different.

DUNCAN GROUPING		Mean	N	Group
	A	0.37	24	Coastal
B	A	0.05	46	Highland
B		-0.35	32	Merina

Alpha = 0.10   DF = 99   MSE = 0.945315
Means with the same letter are not significantly different.

DUNCAN GROUPING	Mean	N	Group
A	0.37	24	Coastal
A	0.05	46	Highland
B	-0.35	32	Merina

Uncertainty Avoidance Index. The selected indicators of Uncertainty Avoidance Index (UAI) are presented in Appendix (Table A2). According to Table 9, the ANOVA procedure suggests that the UAI of the three cultural groups' members are not significantly different at the 0.10 significance level.

Table 9: The output of ANOVA Procedure: differences in UAI (KRAOMA)

DUNCAN's multiple range test for variable: "Uncertainty Avoidance Index"

Alpha = 0.10   DF = 99   MSE = 0.985758
Means with the same letter are not significantly different.

DUNCAN GROUPING	Mean	N	Group
A	0.19	46	Highland
A	-0.08	24	Coastal
A	-0.22	32	Merina

Masculinity Orientation Index. The considered indicators of Masculinity Orientation Index (MAS) are shown in Appendix

(Table A3). The ANOVA procedure in Table 10 shows that at the 0.10 significance level, Coastalers' average MAS is significantly different from those of the Highlanders and the Merina.

Table 10: The output of ANOVA Procedure: differences in MAS (KRAOMA)

DUNCAN's multiple range test for variable: "Masculinity Orientation Index"

Alpha = 0.10 DF = 99 MSE = 0.976042
Means with the same letter are not significantly different.

DUNCAN GROUPING	Mean	N	Group
A	0.37	24	Coastal
B	-0.11	46	Highland
B	-0.12	32	Merina

Group Orientation Index. The chosen indicators of Group Orientation Index (GIND) are presented in Appendix (Table A4). According to the ANOVA procedure in Table 11, at the 0.10 significance level, the GIND of the three cultural groups' members are not significantly different.

Table 11: The output of ANOVA Procedure: differences in GIND (KRAOMA)

DUNCAN's multiple range test for variable: "Group Orientation Index"

Alpha = 0.10 DF = 99 MSE = 1.017616
Means with the same letter are not significantly different.

DUNCAN GROUPING	Mean	N	Group
A	0.07	32	Merina
A	-0.01	46	Highland
A	-0.07	24	Coastal

Task Orientation Index. The selected indicators of Task Orientation Index (TAS) are given in Appendix (Table A6). The ANOVA procedure in Table 12 suggests that the Highlanders' average TAS is significantly different from those of the Coastalers and the Merina at the 0.05 significance level.

Table 12: The output of ANOVA Procedure: differences in TAS (KRAOMA)

DUNCAN's multiple range test for variable: "Task Orientation Index"

Alpha = 0.05   DF = 99   MSE = 0.939979
Means with the same letter are not significantly different.

DUNCAN GROUPING	Mean	N	Group
A	0.29	24	Coastal
A	0.22	32	Merina
B	-0.31	46	Highland

Space Orientation Index. The considered indicators of Space Orientation Index (SPA) are shown in Appendix (Table A5). Table 13, the requested statistic output from the ANOVA procedure, shows that the Coastalers' average SPA is significantly different from that of the Merina at the 0.01 significance level.

Table 13: The output of ANOVA Procedure: differences in SPA (KRAOMA)

DUNCAN's multiple range test for variable: "Space Orientation Index"

Alpha = 0.01   DF = 99   MSE = 0.948581
Means with the same letter are not significantly different.

DUNCAN GROUPING		Mean	N	Group
	A	0.35	32	Merina
B	A	-0.05	46	Highland
B		-0.36	24	Coastal

Human Relation Orientation Index. The chosen indicators of Human Relation Orientation Index (HUM) are presented in Appendix (Table A7). The ANOVA procedure in Table 14 indicates that the average HUM of the three cultural groups' members is not significantly different at the 0.10 significance level.

Table 14: The output of ANOVA Procedure: differences in HUM (KRAOMA)

DUNCAN's multiple range test for variable: "Human Relation Orientation Index"

Alpha = 0.10   DF = 99   MSE = 1.011297
Means with the same letter are not significantly different.

DUNCAN GROUPING	Mean	N	Group
A	0.11	32	Merina
A	0.04	24	Coastal
A	-0.10	46	Highland

Summary. Table 15 summarizes the cultural diversity measurement. In brief, it indicates that the three cultural groups are really culturally diverse since their PDI, MAS, TAS, and SPA are significantly different.

Table 15: Summary of the measurement of cultural diversity (KRAOMA)

Differences	Coastalers	Highlanders	Merina
Coastalers		TAS** MAS*	SPA*** MAS* PDI***
Highlanders			PDI* TAS**
Merina			

*$p<0.10$ **$p<0.05$ ***$p<0.01$

5.3.4. Hypotheses Testing

5.3.4.1. Hypotheses on the Effects of Cultural Distances

Table 18: Output of CALIS procedure: standardized coefficients in regard to differences in PDI, MAS, TAS, and SPA

KRAOMA	Standardized coefficients for:		
Paths with difference in:	Coastal (C)	Highland (H)	Merina (M)
PDI			
p1	-0.1293	-0.2343*	-0.4386***
p2	-0.3452**	-0.1177	-0.3354**
p3	-0.5759***	0.0628	0.1829
p4	-0.0962	-0.3532***	0.0038
p5	-0.1039	0.1449	0.5351***
p6	-0.1006	0.1896	0.4558***
p7	-0.1564	0.2375**	0.3513**
p8	-0.0003	0.2552**	0.4005**
p9	0.2975*	0.2499**	0.4329***
p10	-0.0793	0.2794**	0.1992
MAS			
p1	0.0930	0.0970	0.0813
p2	0.3448**	0.2482**	0.3339**
p3	-0.2462	-0.1043	0.1141
p4	-0.2354	0.0356	0.0354
p5	-0.0059	0.1308	0.4835***
p6	0.1833	0.2137*	0.3835***
p7	-0.1488	0.2365*	0.3419**
p8	-0.0003	0.2552**	0.4002**
p9	0.2975*	0.2499**	0.4335***
p10	-0.0793	0.2794**	0.1990
TAS			
p1	-0.1005	-0.1642	-0.1445
p2	0.8221***	-0.1617	-0.1295
p3	-0.8400***	-0.1624	0.1418
p4	0.1467	-0.1909*	0.0008
p5	-0.1118	0.1111	0.4913***
p6	0.7881**	0.1685	0.4463***
p7	-0.0794	0.1968*	0.3458**
p8	-0.0003	0.2553**	0.3996**
p9	0.2975*	0.2500**	0.4327***
p10	-0.0793	0.2795**	0.1985
SPA			
p1	0.2676*	0.1262	-0.4224***
p2	0.1272	-0.3671***	-0.5420***
p3	0.5323***	0.0708	0.1037
p4	-0.1549	-0.0709	-0.2687*
p5	-0.1716	0.1083	0.4783***
p6	0.0304	0.2227*	0.4652***
p7	-0.0296	0.2353*	0.2731*
p8	-0.0003	0.2552**	0.4023**
p9	0.2975*	0.2499**	0.4354***
p10	-0.0793	0.2794**	0.1998

*p<0.10 **p<0.05 ***p<0.01

HYPOTHESIS 1a: Cultural distances between the cultural groups will affect their success sharing.

Here, we are dealing with the path p1 (Figure 7). According to the CALIS procedure (Table 16), the effect of differences in:
1. PDI on success sharing is significant for:
    - The Highlanders (at the 0.10 level);
    - The Merina (at the 0.01 level);
2. SPA on success sharing is significant for:
    - The Coastalers (at the 0.10 level);
    - The Merina (at the 0.01 level).

That is to say, HYPOTHESIS 1a can be **accepted**.

HYPOTHESIS 1b: The effect of cultural distances on success sharing will not be the same for all of the cultural groups.

While keeping our eyes on the path p1 (Table 16), one would remark that:
1. For all of the cultural groups, success sharing is negatively affected by differences in PDI. However, if we look at the standardized coefficients, we would agree that the effect is higher and more significant for the Merina than for the other cultural groups.
2. To the Coastalers, differences in SPA positively and significantly affect the success sharing; whereas, to the Merina, it is the entire opposite.

In other words, HYPOTHESIS 1b can be **accepted**.

HYPOTHESIS 2a: Cultural distances between the cultural groups will affect their mental models sharing.

Here, we are concerned with the path p2 (Figure 7).

According to the CALIS procedure (Table 16), the effect of differences in:
1. PDI on mental models sharing is significant for:
   - The Coastalers (at the 0.05 level);
   - The Merina (at the 0.05 level);
2. MAS on mental models sharing is significant for all of the cultural groups (at the 0.05 level);
3. TAS on mental models sharing is significant for the Coastalers (at the 0.01 level);
4. SPA on mental models sharing is significant for:
   - The Highlanders (at the 0.01 level);
   - The Merina (at the 0.01 level).

In brief, HYPOTHESIS 2a can be **accepted**.

HYPOTHESIS 2b: The effect of cultural distances on mental models sharing will not be the same for all of the cultural groups.

When we look at the CALIS procedure (Table 16) and consider the rows corresponding to the path p2, one would notice that:
1. Though the effect of differences in PDI on mental models sharing is significantly negative in regard to the Coastalers and the Merina, it is not so in regard to the Highlanders;
2. Though the effect of differences in TAS on mental models sharing is significantly positive in regard to the Coastalers, it is not so in regard to the Highlanders and the Merina;
3. Though the effect of differences in SPA on mental models sharing is significantly negative in regard to the Merina and the Highlanders, it is not so in regard to the Coastalers.

Thus, HYPOTHESIS 2b can be **accepted**.

> HYPOTHESIS 3a: Cultural distances between the cultural groups will affect their vision sharing.

Concerning the path p3 (Figure 7), Table 16 shows that, for the Coastalers, the effects of differences in PDI, TAS, and SPA on vision sharing are significant at the 0.01 level.
In other words, HYPOTHESIS 3a can be **accepted**.

> HYPOTHESIS 3b: The effect of cultural distances on vision sharing will not be the same for all of the cultural groups.

According to the CALIS procedure (Table 16):
1. Though the effects of differences in PDI and TAS on vision sharing are significantly negative in regard to the Coastalers, they are not so in regard to the other cultural groups;
2. Though the effect of differences in SPA on vision sharing is significantly positive in regard to the Coastalers, it is not so in regard to the other cultural groups.

Therefore, HYPOTHESIS 3b can be **accepted**.

> HYPOTHESIS 4a: Cultural distances between the cultural groups will affect their core competence development.

Consider the path p4, as it is shown on Figure 7. The CALIS procedure (Table 16) says that the effect of differences in:
1. PDI on core competence development is significant for the Highlanders at the 0.01 level;
2. TAS on core competence development is significant for the Highlanders at the 0.10 level;
3. SPA on core competence development is significant for the Merina at the 0.10 level.

That is to say, HYPOTHESIS 4a can be **accepted**.

HYPOTHESIS 4b: The effect of cultural distances on core competence development will not be the same for all of the cultural groups.

According to Table 16 (consider the rows corresponding to the path p4):
1. The effects of differences in PDI and TAS on core competence development are significantly negative in regard to the Highlanders, whereas they are not so in regard to the other cultural groups;
2. Though the effect of differences in SPA on core competence development is negative to all of the cultural groups, it is higher and significant in regard to the Merina.

Hence, HYPOTHESIS 4b can be **accepted**.

5.3.4.2. Hypotheses on the Conditions for an Effective Multicultural Management

In order to make the book readable and to keep its volume reasonable, all the figures related to this section would not be presented. Nevertheless, these figures are available and can be provided anytime that they would be required.

Table 17: Summary of the REG procedure (KRAOMA)

	Parameter estimates for:			
	Coastal	Highland	Merina	Together
Dep. Var.: Open and equal opportunity				
Intercep	2.985058***	3.134236***	2.526751***	2.962133***
Training	0.021612	-0.024363	-0.034517	-0.022642
Job performance evaluation feedback	-0.065002	0.194248	-0.059275	0.045053
Job performance eval. transparency	-0.174871	-0.171998	0.208772	-0.070636
Dep. Var.: Success sharing				
Intercep	1.131343*	3.407586***	3.311927***	2.963222***
Open & equal opportunity	1.053731***	0.134623	0.151376	0.268622***
Dep. Var.: Communication				
Intercep	19.07923***	9.850441***	6.122185***	9.423111***
Repeated interactions & social networks	0.021013	0.547795***	0.781606***	0.569790***
Dep. Var.: Conflicts				
Intercep	6.096796	13.70189***	21.80287***	16.22369***
Repeated interactions & social networks	0.560455	0.090552	-0.386251*	-0.036975
Dep. Var.: Mutual understanding				
Intercep	2.38133***	2.063291***	0.510241	1.344608***
Repeated interactions & social networks	0.062005	0.083547**	0.163776***	0.119709***
Dep. Var.: Mutual trust and respect				
Intercep	3.099897	4.803376***	4.494154***	4.612235***
Repeated interactions & social networks	0.243886**	0.183119***	0.201522***	0.185711***
Dep. Var.: Mental models sharing				
Intercep	5.865536	-0.218248	-0.094228	0.085134
Communication	-0.112122	0.071010	0.036871	0.054692
Mutual understanding	-0.174597	0.369815**	-0.096951	0.174925
Mutual trust & respect	-0.081920	0.069884	0.321309	0.138719*
Dep. Var.: Vision sharing				
Intercep	3.126821***	2.46258***	-0.063657	1.76205***
Success sharing	-0.019495	0.133113	0.50790***	0.172931*
Mental models sharing	0.111430	0.210744	0.456148**	0.34809***
Dep. Var.: Higher-level learning				
Intercep	7.918430***	4.68238***	5.85357***	5.44809***
Vision sharing	-0.209781	0.327271	0.67859**	0.414574**
Lower-level learning	-0.039832	0.079700*	-0.081642	-0.002473
Dep. Var.: Satisfaction				
Intercep	48.21712***	38.7395***	37.5005***	40.97834***
Higher-level learning	-0.001335	1.350877*	1.677498**	1.083755**
Dep. Var.: Improvement				
Intercep	17.4708***	19.1259***	15.1014***	17.00852***
Higher-level learning	0.771696	0.789474*	1.096993**	0.948390***
Dep. Var.: Willingness to co-succeed				
Intercep	32.3997***	28.6300***	29.3385***	29.90628***
Higher-level learning	-0.129506	0.649123*	0.393307	0.367711*

t-test: *$p<0.10$ **$p<0.05$ ***$p<0.01$

Success Sharing.

> HYPOTHESIS 5: All employees from all cultural backgrounds will recognize that the more training they receive, the more open and equal their opportunity to succeed and be promoted will be.

According to the REG procedure (Table 17), the Highlanders and the Merina seem not to confirm this hypothesis because, for these cultural groups, the parameter estimates of the independent variable "training" are negative.

Figures 13 and 14, however, indicate that, though a fluctuation appears in the middle of each curve, the figures would confirm the hypothesis before and after the fluctuation.

Figure 13: The relationship between training and equal opportunity to succeed and be promoted according to the Coastalers at KRAOMA

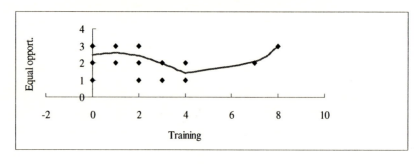

Figure 14: The relationship between training and equal opportunity to succeed and be promoted according to the Merina at KRAOMA

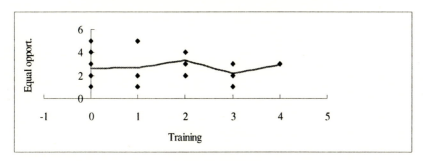

In other words, they would suggest that the more training the employees will get, the more open and equal their opportunity to succeed and be promoted will be, though a temporary turbulence may occur in the course of time. That is, with the figures, HYPOTHESIS 5 could be **accepted**.

> HYPOTHESIS 6: All employees from all cultural backgrounds will recognize that the more job performance evaluation feedback they receive, the more open and equal their opportunities to succeed and be promoted will be.

The output of the REG procedure (Table 17) suggests that the Coastalers and the Merina do not confirm the hypothesis because, for these cultural groups, the parameter estimates of the independent variable "feedback" are negative.

According to Figures 15 and 16, however, each curve's slope is positive (though that of the Coastalers appears to be near to zero at the beginning), thus, appears to support the hypothesis. Therefore, based upon the figures, HYPOTHESIS 6 could also be **accepted**.

Figure 15: The relationship between job performance evaluation feedback and equal opportunity to succeed and be promoted according to the Coastalers at KRAOMA

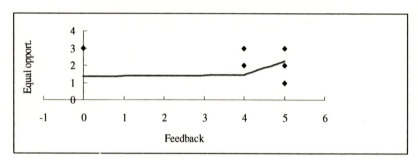

Figure 16: The relationship between job performance evaluation feedback and equal opportunity to succeed and be promoted according to the Merina at KRAOMA

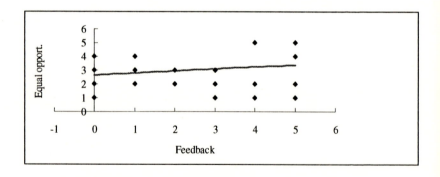

HYPOTHESIS 7: All employees from all cultural backgrounds will recognize that the more job performance evaluation is transparent, the more open and equal their opportunity to succeed and be promoted will be.

According to Figures 17-19, this hypothesis could be

accepted, since:
1. When job performance evaluation would become regularly transparent, the slope of the curve for the Coastalers (Figure 17) and the Highlanders (Figure 18) would also become positive.
2. Together, the sampled employees support the hypothesis because the slope of their curve is positive (Figure 19).

Figure 17: The relationship between job performance evaluation transparency and equal opportunity to succeed and be promoted according to the Coastalers at KRAOMA

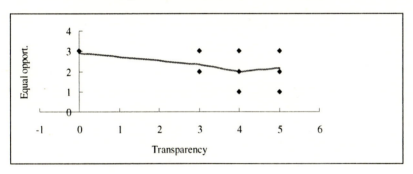

Figure 18: The relationship between job performance evaluation transparency and equal opportunity to succeed and be promoted according to the Highlanders at KRAOMA

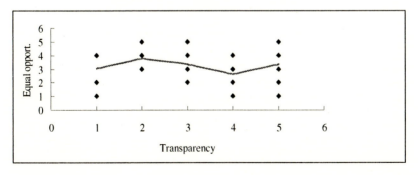

Figure 19: The relationship between job performance evaluation transparency and equal opportunity to succeed and be promoted according to the sampled employees at KRAOMA

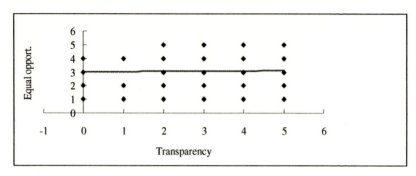

HYPOTHESIS 8: All employees from all cultural backgrounds will recognize that the more their opportunities to succeed and be promoted are open and equal, the more success sharing there will be.

According to the REG procedure (Table 17), all of the cultural groups appear to support this hypothesis because the parameter estimates of the independent variable "open and equal opportunity" are positive. Moreover, Figures 20-22 present curves with positive slopes. Therefore, with the REG procedure and the figures, HYPOTHESIS 8 could be **accepted**.

Figure 20: The relationship between equal opportunity to succeed and be promoted and success sharing according to the Coastalers at KRAOMA

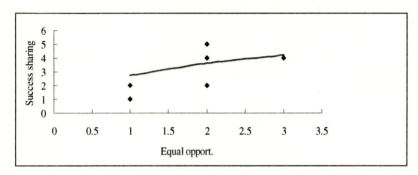

Figure 21: The relationship between equal opportunity to succeed and be promoted and success sharing according to the Highlanders at KRAOMA

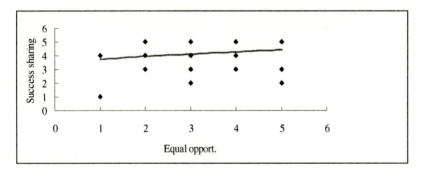

Figure 22: The relationship between equal opportunity to succeed and be promoted and success sharing according to the Merina at KRAOMA

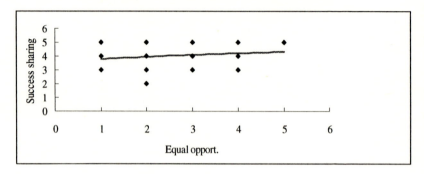

Mental Models Sharing.

> HYPOTHESIS 9: All employees from all cultural backgrounds will recognize that the more repeated interactions and social networks there are, the better their communication will be.

The output of the REG procedure (Table 17) suggests that the parameter estimates for all of the cultural groups are positive.

Like Figures 20-22, the related figures (which show the relationship between repeated interactions and social networks and communication) indicate that the cultural groups' related curves have positive slopes.

In other words, with the REG procedure and the figures, HYPOTHESIS 9 could be **accepted**.

HYPOTHESIS 10: All employees from all cultural backgrounds will recognize that the more repeated interactions and social networks there are, the less conflicts there will be.

The output of the REG procedure (Table 17) indicates that the Coastalers and the Highlanders do not support this hypothesis since the parameter estimates of the independent variable "repeated interactions and social networks" are positive for these cultural groups. In addition, Figures 23-25 are consistent with the REG procedure because all of the slopes of the curves are positive. In other words, HYPOTHESIS 10 could be **rejected**.

Figure 23: The relationship between repeated interactions and social networks and non-constructive conflicts according to the Coastalers at KRAOMA

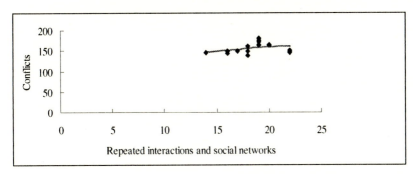

Figure 24: The relationship between repeated interactions and social networks and non-constructive conflicts according to the Highlanders at KRAOMA

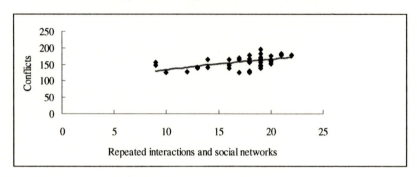

Figure 25: The relationship between repeated interactions and social networks and non-constructive conflicts according to the Merina at KRAOMA

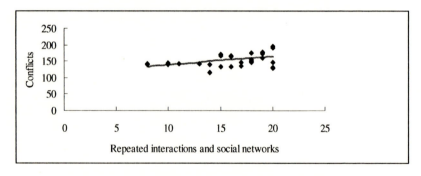

HYPOTHESIS 11: All employees from all cultural backgrounds will recognize that the more repeated interactions and social networks there are, the more they will understand each other.

The REG procedure (Table 17) suggests that, all of the cultural groups confirm the hypothesis because the parameter estimates of the independent variable "repeated interactions and social networks" are positive for all of the cultural groups. In addition, the related figures (which show the relationship between repeated interactions and social networks and mutual understanding) have similar tendency to Figures 23-25—that is, indicate curves with positive slopes.

Thus, based upon the REG procedure and the figures, HYPOTHESIS 11 could be **accepted**.

> HYPOTHESIS 12: All employees from all cultural backgrounds will recognize that the more repeated interactions and social networks there are, the more they will trust and respect each other.

The output of the REG procedure (Table 17) shows that all of the cultural groups significantly support the hypothesis.

The related figures (which show the relationship between repeated interactions and social networks and mutual trust and respect) are consistent with the REG procedure because, like in Figures 20-22, the slopes of all of the cultural groups' curves are also positive.

In other words, based upon the REG procedure and the figures, HYPOTHESIS 12 could be **accepted**.

> HYPOTHESIS 13: All employees from all cultural backgrounds will recognize that the more repeated interactions and social networks there are, the more cooperation there will be.

This hypothesis has not been tested because many of the Coastalers did not answer or did not answer correctly the questions related to cooperation.

HYPOTHESIS 14: All employees from all cultural backgrounds will recognize that the better their communication is, the more mental models sharing there will be.

According to the REG procedure (Table 17), the Coastalers do not support the hypothesis because the parameter estimate of the independent variable "communication" is negative for this cultural group.

However, if we look at Figure 26, HYPOTHESIS 14 could be **accepted** because, though a fluctuation appears in the middle of the curve for the Coastalers, the slopes of the curve before and after that fluctuation are positive. This would mean that such abnormality could be considered as temporary in the course of time.

Figure 26: The relationship between quality of communication and mental models sharing according to the Coastalers at KRAOMA

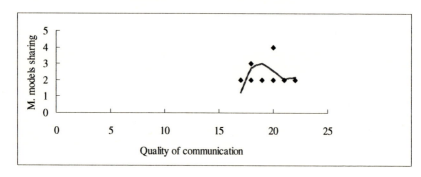

HYPOTHESIS 15: All employees from all cultural backgrounds will recognize that the more they understand each other, the more mental models sharing there will be.

The output of the REG procedure (Table 17) suggests that the Coastalers and the Merina do not confirm the hypothesis because the parameter estimates of the independent variable "mutual understanding" are negative for these cultural groups.

Though Figure 27 seems to be consistent with the REG procedure's output:
1. Figure 28 (related figure for the Merina) shows that the slope of the curve is positive;
2. The last column of Table 17 and Figure 29 indicate that, when considered together, the sampled employees seem to support the hypothesis:
    - The parameter estimate of the independent variable "mutual understanding" is positive;
    - The slope of their curve is positive.

In other words, **HYPOTHESIS 15** could be **discussed**.

Figure 27: The relationship between mutual understanding and mental models sharing according to the Coastalers at KRAOMA

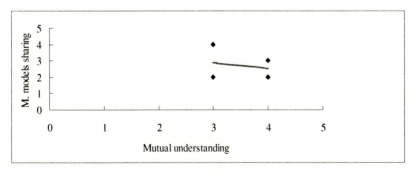

Figure 28: The relationship between mutual understanding
and mental models sharing
according to the Merina at KRAOMA

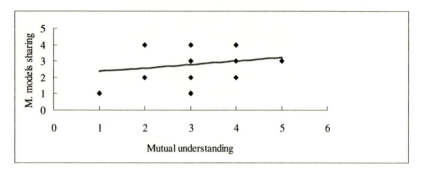

Figure 29: The relationship between mutual understanding
and mental models sharing
according to the sampled employees at KRAOMA

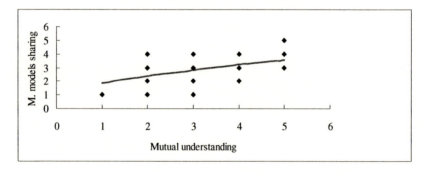

HYPOTHESIS 16: All employees from all cultural backgrounds will recognize that the more they trust and respect each other, the more mental models sharing there will be.

1. The REG procedure (Table 17) indicates that the Coastalers appear not to support the hypothesis, yet when the sampled employees are considered together, the parameter estimate of the independent variable "mutual trust and respect" is positive.
2. Though Figure 30 (related to the Coastalers) appears to confirm the REG procedure's output, Figure 31 (related to the sampled employees) suggests that, when considered together, the sampled employees seem to support the hypothesis.

In a word, HYPOTHESIS 16 could also be **discussed**.

Figure 30: The relationship between mutual trust and respect and mental models sharing according to the Coastalers at KRAOMA

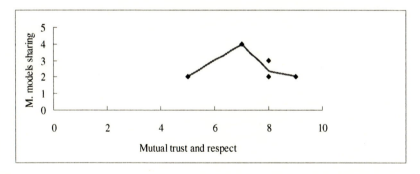

Figure 31: The relationship between mutual trust and respect
and mental models sharing
according to the sampled employees at KRAOMA

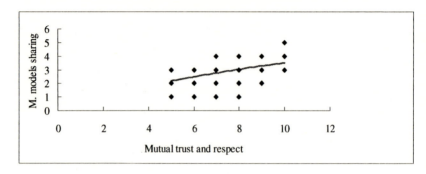

> HYPOTHESIS 17: All employees from all cultural backgrounds will recognize that the more they cooperate, the more mental models sharing there will be.

As for **HYPOTHESIS 13**, this hypothesis has not been tested because many of the Coastalers did not answer or did not answer correctly the questions related to cooperation.

Vision Sharing.

> HYPOTHESIS 18: All employees from all cultural backgrounds will recognize that the more success sharing there is, the more vision sharing there will be.

Consider the path p5 on Figure 7. The output of the CALIS procedure (Table 16) shows that, considering the cultural groups' differences in PDI, MAS, TAS, and SPA:
- The Highlanders and the Merina think that success sharing has a positive impact on vision sharing;
- The Coastalers think the opposite.

The REG procedure's output (Table 17) first appears to be consistent with the CALIS procedure's result since the parameter estimate of the independent variable "success sharing" is negative for the Coastalers. However, if the sampled employees are considered together, without any cultural categorization, Table 17 suggests a positive parameter estimate which supports the hypothesis.

In addition, if we look at the figures which indicate the relationship between success sharing and vision sharing:
1. Figure 32 shows that, in the course of time, the slope of the Coastalers' curve is slightly positive. In other words, it would mean that, within a certain interval of success sharing level, the Coastalers would confirm the hypothesis.
2. Figure 33 suggests that, when considered together, the sampled employees confirm the hypothesis because the slope of their curve is positive.

That is, **HYPOTHESIS 18** could also be **discussed**.

Figure 32: The relationship between success sharing and vision sharing according to the Coastalers at KRAOMA

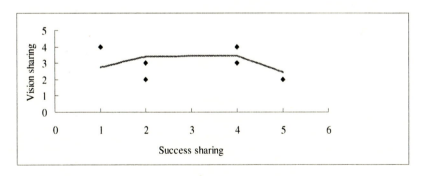

Figure 33: The relationship between success sharing
and vision sharing
according to the sampled employees at KRAOMA

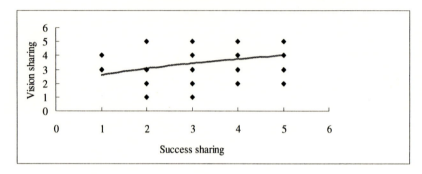

HYPOTHESIS 19: All employees from all cultural backgrounds will recognize that the more mental models sharing there is, the more vision sharing there will be.

Consider the path p6 (Figure 7). In regard to the cultural groups' differences in PDI, the CALIS procedure's output (Table 16) shows that, the Coastalers do not confirm the hypothesis.

The output of the REG procedure (Table 17) and the related figures (which have similar tendencies to Figures 20-22), however, affirm that all of the cultural groups confirm the hypothesis.

In other words, based upon the REG procedure and the figures, HYPOTHESIS 19 could be **accepted.**

Core Competence Development.

> HYPOTHESIS 20: All employees from all cultural backgrounds will recognize that the more vision sharing there is, the more core competence development there will be.

Concerning the path p7 (Figure 7), the output of the CALIS procedure (Table 16) shows that the standardized coefficients for the Coastalers are negative in regard to all cultural dimensions.

The output of the REG procedure (Table 17) first appears to support the CALIS procedure's result by showing that the parameter estimate of the independent variable "core competence development" is negative for the Coastalers. However, if the sample employees are considered together, Table 17 suggests a positive parameter estimate for the independent variable.

Moreover, the figures showing the relationship between vision sharing and core competence development have similar tendencies to Figures 20-22. That is, all of the cultural groups confirm the hypothesis because all of the slopes of their curves are positive.

Thus, based upon the figures, HYPOTHESIS 20 could be **accepted**.

> HYPOTHESIS 21: All employees from all cultural backgrounds will recognize that their higher-level learning is directly related to their lower-level learning success.

According to the output of the REG procedure (Table 17), the Coastalers and the Merina appear to deny the hypothesis because the parameter estimates of the independent variable "lower-level learning" are negative for these cultural groups.

However, the related figures show that **HYPOTHESIS 21** could be **discussed.** Indeed:
1. The Coastalers' curve has a positive slope (Figure 34);
2. To a certain degree of lower-level learning, the Merina's curve has a positive slope (Figure 35);
3. As a whole, the sample employees' curve has a positive slope (Figure 36).

Figure 34: The relationship between lower-level learning and higher-level learning according to the Coastalers at KRAOMA

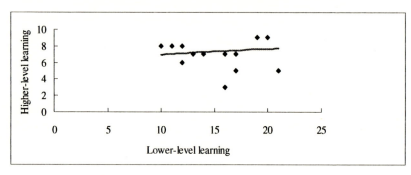

Figure 35: The relationship between lower-level learning
and higher-level learning
according to the Merina at KRAOMA

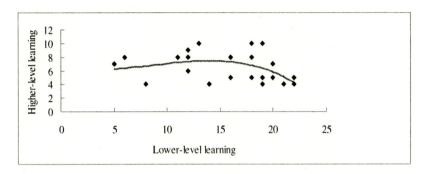

Figure 36: The relationship between lower-level learning
and higher-level learning
according to the sampled employees at KRAOMA

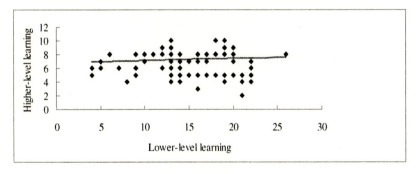

5.3.4.3. Hypotheses on the Linkage Between Core Competence Development and Performance

HYPOTHESIS 22: All employees from all cultural backgrounds will recognize that the more they develop their core competence, the more satisfaction they will have.

Consider the path p8 on Figure 7. According to the output of the CALIS procedure (Table 16), the effect of core competence development on members' satisfaction is positive for the Highlanders and the Merina, whereas, it is slightly negative for the Coastalers. This result is consistent with the result of the REG procedure (Table 17) which suggests that the parameter estimate of the independent variable "core competence development" is negative for the Coastalers. If the sample employees are, however, considered as a whole, Table 17 indicates a positive and significant (at 0.05 level) parameter estimate for the independent variable.

Moreover, the related figures have similar tendencies to Figures 20-22. Thus, all of the curves' slopes are positive.

In other words, considering the figures, HYPOTHESIS 22 could be **accepted**.

> HYPOTHESIS 23: All employees from all cultural backgrounds will recognize that the more they develop their core competence, the more improvement there will be.

Concerning the path p9 on Figure 7, the output of the CALIS procedure (Table 16) suggests that the effect of core competence development on improved areas is significantly positive for all of the cultural groups. In other words, HYPOTHESIS 23 can be **accepted**.

> HYPOTHESIS 24: All employees from all cultural backgrounds will recognize that the more they develop their core competence, the more they will be willing to co-succeed.

Considering the path p10 on Figure 7, the output of the

CALIS procedure (Table 16) suggests that, the standardized coefficients for the Coastalers are negative.

The output of the REG procedure (Table 17) first appears to be consistent with the CALIS procedure's result, because it indicates that the parameter estimate of the independent variable "core competence development" is negative for the Coastalers. However, when the sampled employees are considered together, Table 17 presents a positive and significant (at the 0.10 level) parameter estimate for the independent variable.

Also, according to the related figures, **HYPOTHESIS 24** could be **accepted** because:
1. The slopes of the Coastalers and the Merina's curves will be positive when core competence development will become common and frequent at the workplace (Figures 37 and 38 respectively).

Figure 37: The relationship between core competence development and willingness to co-succeed according to the Coastalers at KRAOMA

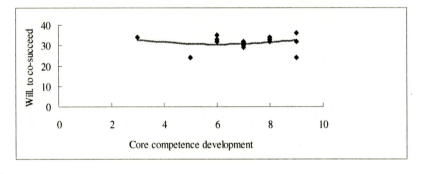

Figure 38: The relationship between core competence development and willingness to co-succeed according to the Merina at KRAOMA

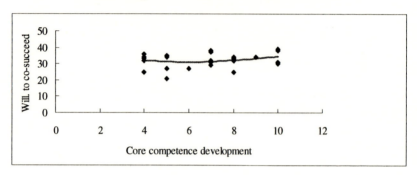

2. When considered together, the sample employees appear to support the hypothesis because the slope of their curve is also positive (Figure 39).

Figure 39: The relationship between core competence development and willingness to co-succeed according to the sampled employees at KRAOMA

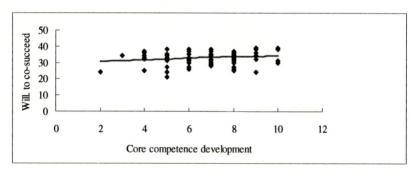

5.3.5. Interpretations, Findings, and Discussions

The specific results of the hypotheses testing are as follows:

1. As it was expected, all the hypotheses concerning the effects of cultural distances on success sharing, mental models sharing, vision sharing, and core competence development have been accepted. In other words, the Coastalers, the Highlanders, and the Merina's cultural distances do really matter at KRAOMA, so that they have to be carefully considered.
   This result also supports the statement that cultural diversity does influence management practices and its impacts can be identified in the motivational, the interaction, the visioning, and the learning processes.

2. Furthermore, the results show that the effects of cultural distances on success sharing, mental models sharing, vision sharing, and core competence development are not the same for all of the cultural groups. This indicates that when the different cultural groups interact in the workplace some of them would likely be found *more negatively* affected by the differences in a given specific dimension of culture content (PDI or MAS or TAS or SPA). And, thereby, they would likely impede the integration and combination of the employees' ideas and competencies, attitudes and behaviors, ways of thinking and doing ...

Table 18: The most negatively affected cultural groups
in regard to differences in PDI, MAS, TAS, and SPA (KRAOMA)

Concerning	MOSTLY affected cultural groups	PDI	MAS	TAS	SPA
Success sharing	Merina	X			X
Mental Models sharing	Coastal	X			
	Merina				X
Vision sharing	Coastal	X		X	
Higher-level learning	Highland	X		X	
	Merina				X

Table 18 shows that, regarding the effect of:
- Differences in PDI and SPA on success sharing, the Merina would be found to be the most negatively affected;
- Differences in PDI on mental models sharing, the Coastalers and the Merina would be both identified to be the most negatively affected;
- Differences in SPA on mental models sharing, the Merina would be found to be the most negatively affected;
- Differences in PDI and TAS on vision sharing, the Coastalers would be found to be the most negatively affected;
- Differences in PDI and TAS on core competence development, the Highlanders would be identified to be the most negatively affected;
- Differences in SPA on core competence development, the Merina would be found to be the most negatively affected.

From Table 18 also one would remark that the Highlanders are only mentioned to be the most negatively affected when the effect of differences in PDI and TAS on core competence development is considered. Undoubtedly, this is consistent with the Highlanders':
- Intermediate cultural position in regard to those of the Coastalers and the Merina (Table 19);
- TAS—lowest standardized mean (Table 12).

3. According to Table 19, the Coastalers and the Merina appear to be the two antagonistic cultural groups, whereas the Highlanders seem to hold a strategic cultural position between them. Therefore, it might be possible that the Highlanders would have:
- Intermediate and impartial attitudes, behaviors, way of thinking, way of doing ...;
- The potential to:
  - Play the role of cultural[23] and functional interface[24];
  - Be the promoter of multicultural learning at KRAOMA.

Table 19: The cultural groups' cultural positions (KRAOMA)

Cultural Dimensions	Positions
Power Distance Index	Coastal > *Highland* > Merina (0.37) (0.05) (-0.35)
Masculinity Orientation	Coastal > *Highland* > Merina (0.37) (-0.10) (-0.12)
Task Orientation	Coastal > Merina > Highland (0.29) (0.22) (-0.31)
Space Orientation	Merina > *Highland* > Coastal (0.35) (-0.05) (-0.36)

* **(Standardized mean)**

4. According to Table 20:
- Power/dominance discrepancies exist between the cultural groups;
- The Merina (dominant group) hold advantages in power/dominance and economic resource;
- The Coastalers hold the second position in occupational positions and wages.

---

[23] *Cultural Interface* involves communication interface.
[24] This concept is a development of that of Hayashi (1985) (see **Chapter 2**). The difference between the two notions is that, here, the cultural and functional interfaces are members of a group that is different from the antagonistic ones.

Table 20: The cultural groups' power/dominance positions (KRAOMA)

Power/Dominance	Positions
Occupational Position	Merina > Coastal > Highland (2.00) (1.29) (1.17)
Wage	Merina > Coastal > Highland (6.38) (6.17) (5.35)
Educational Level	Merina > Highland > Coastal (3.25) (3.07) (2.92)

* **(Standardized mean)**

Regarding the power/dominance discrepancies and the satisfaction levels of the Coastalers and the Highlanders (Table 21), it seems that:

1. The Highlanders feel less dissatisfied than their counterparts Coastalers and prefer to be content with the status quo. Indeed, their power/dominance position appears not to allow them to enter in a contest and conquer the highest position. This is what one would call *a feeling of resignation.*
2. On the contrary, the Coastalers feel more discomfort because their current power/dominance position seems to allow them to hope and contend for a better/higher position (that is why they cry out for open and equal opportunity). This is what one would name *a feeling of challenge.*
3. The Merina are the most satisfied group because they hold the highest power/dominance position and, hypothetically, the more a group holds the power, the more this group is satisfied. They have what one would describe as *a feeling of contentment.*

Table 21: The cultural groups' satisfaction levels (KRAOMA)

Cultural Groups	Satisfaction Levels
Merina Group	21.31
Highland Group	*19.37*
Coastal Group	18.88

* Each group: 17 items
* 1 item: Not at all (1) - Very satisfied (5)

Here, the Highlanders' feeling confirms the above-mentioned view of this group members' potentiality to play the roles of cultural and functional interfaces. Indeed, since they seem to accept to resign the race for higher power/dominance positions, they would likely put themselves out of any potential unlearning situation (e.g., due to dispute or destructive conflict)[25] and, thereby, incite a more flexible and dynamic climate (e.g., favored by constructive conflict) which would welcome multicultural learning.

Nevertheless, Cox (1993) asserts that if power/dominance discrepancies/imbalances persist too long, then they may have the effect of reducing the motivation and the perceived opportunity among members of non-dominant groups to participate and to excel in their fullest potential in diverse-group setting. Hence, the importance of seeking more balanced representation and power among the cultural groups.

5. HYPOTHESIS 10 has been rejected because all the cultural groups' members rather tend to view repeated interactions and social networks as factors leading to conflicts. This result:
* Seems to hint the existence of hostility between the cultural groups' members. Indeed, beyond the historical background of the island:

---

[25] According to Table 17, the Highland group members view conflict as a factor impeding mental models sharing (significant at the 0.10 level).

- ✓ Many of their viewpoints are significantly opposite from each other (Table 17);
- ✓ As mentioned earlier, the cultural groups' cultures, power/dominance positions, satisfaction levels, and feelings toward the status quo are different from each other (Tables 19-21).
- Is congruent with Figure 40 which shows that difference in cultural group (regional origin) is the major source of conflict at KRAOMA (total score = 151). On average, all of the sample employees affirm that conflicts due to cultural group differences happen in the firm, at least, rarely. Figure 41 indicates that, among the 72 employees in the sample (79.59%) who assert this fact:
    - ✓ 11 employees (15.28%) state that conflicts occur rarely;
    - ✓ 43 employees (59.72%) affirm that conflicts happen occasionally;
    - ✓ 18 employees (25.00%) declare that conflicts are frequent.

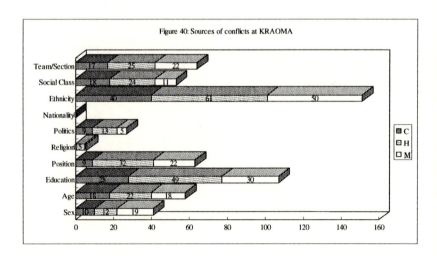

Figure 40: Sources of conflicts at KRAOMA

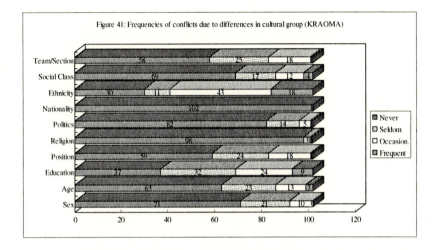

Figure 41: Frequencies of conflicts due to differences in cultural group (KRAOMA)

6. Though HYPOTHESIS 15 and HYPOTHESIS 16 have not been accepted (because the Coastalers do not agree that more mutual understanding and more mutual trust and respect would lead to more mental models sharing), they can be subject of discussions because when considered together, the sample employees support the hypotheses.

Indeed, apparently, these results seem to indicate that, though the Coastalers' viewpoint appears to be pessimistic, their point of view is rather weakened or even shifted when they are together with the other cultural groups who support the hypotheses. This suggests that the presence and interactions of culturally diverse workforce at the workplace could bring contextual change and dynamism among the cultural groups. As a result, everybody would not likely be stuck with his/her own ideas, viewpoints, ways of thinking, and so on.

7. HYPOTHESIS 18 also can be subject of discussion because, though the slope of the Coastalers' curve (Figure 32) is only positive to some degree of success sharing:

- The result does not suggest that the Coastalers entirely disagree with the hypothesis;
- The REG procedure and Figure 33 indicate that, when considered together, the sample employees support the hypothesis.

If the second reason could just be interpreted as a change or a shift in the Coastalers' viewpoint when they are together with the other cultural groups' members, then, with point 5., one could deduce that:
1. The conceptual model is suitable for a multicultural workforce;
2. **HYPOTHESES 15, 16** and **18** could be accepted at the multicultural level.

8. HYPOTHESIS 21 has not been accepted because, from a certain degree of lower-level learning, the Merina's curve has a negative slope. Maybe they think that though training is granted to the employees, it seems not to help them to progress to develop their core competence. Indeed, on average, all of the cultural groups agree on the helplessness and the inadequacy of the employees' training to their current responsibilities (Table 22).

Table 22: The sample employees' training usefulness in their current works (KRAOMA)

Level = 0: not applicable
Level = 1: Not helpful at all
Level = 2: A little helpful
Level = 3: Uncertain
Level = 4: Helpful
Level = 5: Very helpful

	Mean
Coastalers	2.63
Highlanders	2.28
Merina	2.72
Sampled employees	2.50

That is, if training would be available at the proper time and suitable for the employees' current activities, tasks, and responsibilities, then, probably the hypothesis would be easily accepted.

9. Table 23 summarizes the result of the hypotheses testing:

Table 23: Result of the hypotheses testing with KRAOMA's data

Hypotheses on:	Accepted	Discussed	Rejected	Not Tested	Total
1. Effects of Cultural Distances	8				8
2. The Conditions for an Effective Multicultural Management	10	4	1	2	17
3. The Linkage between Core Competence and Performance	3				3
TOTAL	21	4	1	2	28

Though the feature of the result appears to suggest the consistency and the suitability of the framework, here, it would be argued that, if the Highlanders would contribute and efficiently play the role of cultural and functional interfaces:

1. This framework would smooth out;
2. Multicultural workforce's balance would be reached;
3. KRAOMA's situation could be ameliorated/improved.

5.4. STAR

5.4.1. Responses to Questionnaires

An initial request of the 150 employees in the sample yielded 105 responses (70.00%). However, 2 employees did not answer the key-questions and/or did not answer them correctly. Therefore, those 2 sets of responses were eliminated from the database. That left a sample of 103 responses to be analyzed.

5.4.2. The Sampled Employees

The sample for this study consists of 39 employees from the Coastal group (37.86%), 27 employees from the Highland group (26.21%), and 37 employees from the Merina group (35.92%). The representativeness of this sample was not evaluated since almost all of the companies in Madagascar do not have and do not disclose their personnel data by ethnic group. Therefore, as it has been mentioned above, this fact itself hints and reflects Malagasy companies' naivety and/or unawareness and/or sensitiveness about cultural diversity.

The sample consists of 65 men and 38 women and their average age is between 30 to 39 years old (Table 24).

Table 24: Personal data of STAR's sampled employees

Variable	Mean	Std Dev	Levels
Age	3.51	0.78	5
Contract	1.95	0.22	2
Job Nature	2.74	0.51	3
Type of Pay	2.77	0.42	6
Prior Firms	0.75	1.03	6
Years spent at **STAR**	3.75	1.55	6
Overseas	0.04	0.28	6

Most of the sampled employees (Table 24):
- Have permanent contracts;
- Are performing intellectual jobs;
- Have been paid a fixed monthly salary.

According to Table 24, on average, the sampled employees had already worked for another company before coming to STAR, where they have been working for about 6 to 15 years. Nevertheless, almost all of these employees appear not to have any overseas appointment opportunity.

5.4.3. Measurement of Cultural Diversity

- The correlation coefficients obtained from the CORR procedure indicate that each cultural group members' answers to the questionnaire are significantly different from those of other cultural groups (Table 25);

Table 25: Correlations between each cultural group members' answers to the survey (STAR)

	Coastalers	Highlanders	Merina
Coastalers	1.00000	-0.46528***	-0.58448***
Highlanders		1.00000	-0.44628***
Merina			1.00000

SPEARMAN correlation coefficients; ***p<0.01

- On average, the sample employees are convinced that their team and organizational members do not have similar ethnic and cultural backgrounds, attitude and behavior patterns, values and needs, and way of thinking and doing (Table 26).

Table 26: Similarities of STAR's sampled employees

Level = 1 (lowest)   Very different
Level = 5 (highest) Very similar

Variable	Mean	Std Dev
Ethnic and/or cultural backgrounds	2.35	1.16
Promotion/Success Opportunity	3.14	0.96
Attitude and behavior patterns	2.71	0.98
Values and needs	2.55	1.02
Skills	2.31	0.98
Job Experiences	2.46	1.08
Way of thinking and doing	2.59	1.04

Power Distance. Considering the chosen indicators of Power Distance Index (PDI) in Appendix (Table A1), the statistic output from the ANOVA procedure shows that (Table 27), at the 0.05 significance level, the Merina's average PDI is significantly different from that of the Coastalers.

Table 27: The output of ANOVA procedure: differences in PDI (STAR)

DUNCAN's multiple range test for variable: "Power Distance Index"

Alpha = 0.05   DF = 100   MSE = 0.952982
Means with the same letter are not significantly different.

	DUNCAN GROUPING	Mean	N	Group
	A	0.29	39	Coastal
B	A	0.03	27	Highland
B		-0.30	37	Merina

Uncertainty Avoidance Indexes. The selected indicators of Uncertainty Avoidance Index (UAI) are presented in Appendix (Table A2). According to Table 28, the ANOVA procedure suggests that the UAI of the three cultural groups' members are not significantly different at the 0.10 significance level.

Table 28: The output of ANOVA procedure: differences in UAI (STAR)

DUNCAN's multiple range test for variable: "Uncertainty Avoidance Index"

Alpha = 0.10   DF = 100   MSE = 0.995026
Means with the same letter are not significantly different.

DUNCAN GROUPING	Mean	N	Group
A	0.20	27	Highland
A	0.04	37	Merina
A	-0.18	39	Coastal

Masculinity Orientation Indexes. The considered indicators of

Masculinity Orientation Index (MAS) are shown in Appendix (Table A3). The ANOVA procedure in Table 29 shows that at the 0.10 significance level, Coastalers' average MAS is significantly different from those of the Highlanders and the Merina.

Table 29: The output of ANOVA procedure: differences in MAS (STAR)

DUNCAN's multiple range test for variable: "Masculinity Orientation Index"

Alpha = 0.10   DF = 100   MSE = 0.963192
Means with the same letter are not significantly different.

DUNCAN GROUPING	Mean	N	Group
A	0.19	39	Coastal
B	0.17	27	Highland
B	-0.30	37	Merina

Group Orientation Indexes. The chosen indicators of Group Orientation Index (GIND) are presented in Appendix (Table A4). According to the ANOVA procedure in Table 30, at the 0.10 significance level, the GIND of the three cultural groups' members are not significantly different.

Table 30: The output of ANOVA procedure: differences in GIND (STAR)

DUNCAN's multiple range test for variable: "Group Orientation Index"

Alpha = 0.10   DF = 100   MSE = 0.971738
Means with the same letter are not significantly different.

DUNCAN GROUPING	Mean	N	Group
A	0.18	37	Merina
A	0.14	27	Highland
A	-0.29	39	Coastal

Task Orientation Indexes. The selected indicators of Task Orientation Index (TAS) are given in Appendix (Table A6). The

ANOVA procedure in Table 31 suggests that the Coastalers' average TAS is significantly different from that of the Highlanders at the 0.05 significance level.

Table 31: The output of ANOVA procedure: differences in TAS (STAR)

DUNCAN's multiple range test for variable: "Task Orientation Index"

Alpha = 0.05   DF = 100   MSE = 0.96716
Means with the same letter are not significantly different.

DUNCAN GROUPING		Mean	N	Group
	A	0.28	39	Coastal
B	A	0.09	37	Merina
B		-0.27	27	Highland

Space Orientation Indexes. The considered indicators of Space Orientation Index (SPA) are shown in Appendix (Table A5). Table 32 shows that the Coastalers' average SPA is significantly different from that of the Merina at the 0.10 significance level.

Table 32: The output of ANOVA procedure: differences in SPA (STAR)

DUNCAN's multiple range test for variable: "Space Orientation Index"

Alpha = 0.10   DF = 100   MSE = 0.978624
Means with the same letter are not significantly different.

DUNCAN GROUPING		Mean	N	Group
	A	0.19	39	Coastal
B	A	0.08	27	Highland
B		-0.26	37	Merina

Human Relation Orientation Indexes. The chosen indicators of Human Relation Orientation Index (HUM) are presented in Appendix (Table A7). The ANOVA procedure in Table 33 indicates that the average HUM of the three cultural groups' members is not significantly different at the 0.10 significance level.

Table 33: The output of ANOVA procedure: differences in HUM (STAR)

DUNCAN's multiple range test for variable: "Human Relation Orientation Index"

Alpha = 0.10   DF = 100   MSE = 0.96755
Means with the same letter are not significantly different.

DUNCAN GROUPING	Mean	N	Group
A	0.32	37	Merina
A	0.02	39	Coastal
A	-0.26	27	Highland

Summary. Table 34 summarizes the cultural diversity measurement. In brief, it indicates that the three cultural groups are really culturally diverse since their PDI, MAS, TAS, and SPA are significantly different.

Table 34: Summary of the measurement of cultural diversity (STAR)

Differences	Coastalers	Highlanders	Merina
Coastalers		TAS** MAS*	SPA* MAS* PDI**
Highlanders			PDI*
Merina			

*p<0.10   **p<0.05   ***p<0.01

Quantitative Analysis: The Cases of KRAOMA & STAR

5.4.4. Hypotheses Testing

Table 35: The output of CALIS procedure: standardized coefficients in regard to differences in PDI, MAS, TAS, and SPA

STAR Path with difference in:	Standardized coefficients for:		
	Coastal (C)	Highland (H)	Merina (M)
PDI			
p1	-0.2066	-0.5430***	0.1209
p2	-0.3037**	-0.1024	0.4549***
p3	-0.2476	0.4427*	-0.0748
p4	0.2862	-0.1638*	0.2506**
p5	0.1879	0.5060	0.7604***
p6	-0.0746	0.0417	0.1014
p7	0.5596	0.4810	0.7196*
p8	-2.3601	3.1936***	-0.5102
p9	-0.3672	-6.8596**	1.0931*
p10	-1.5668	0.1577	0.8569*
MAS			
p1	0.2263*	-0.4044**	-0.1083
p2	0.0051	0.0448	0.0748
p3	0.0209	0.3215	0.2191**
p4	0.0800	0.0064	0.1353
p5	0.2181	0.3951	0.8013**
p6	-0.0130	0.0425	0.0348
p7	0.4785	0.4531**	0.7167*
p8	1.5834	-2.8627***	-0.0118
p9	-1.3987	6.8890*	-0.2684
p10	0.6626	0.5991	-1.3482
TAS			
p1	0.0347	-0.0964	-0.2004*
p2	0.0997	0.0802	0.0769
p3	-0.2297**	-0.0650	0.0677
p4	0.0640	0.7103***	0.1320*
p5	0.2268	0.1852	0.7840**
p6	0.0170	0.1766	0.0531
p7	0.4983**	0.5030**	0.7467***
p8	7.7264***	0.5039**	5.2265***
p9	1.6295***	-0.6758**	1.1478
p10	14.5263***	-0.0065	-1.2821
SPA			
p1	-0.1623	-0.1388	0.1256
p2	0.3318**	0.5031**	-0.1399
p3	0.0538	-0.2025	0.0468
p4	0.1606	0.2425*	0.0531
p5	0.2372	0.0786	0.7554**
p6	-0.0289	0.3316	0.0760
p7	0.4831	0.4655	0.7283
p8	-1.6266	0.1281	-0.4619
p9	-0.1558	0.6164	-1.5849
p10	-1.5851	-0.2787	-1.9439

z-test; *p<0.10   **p<0.05   ***p<0.01

5.4.4.1. Hypotheses on the Effects of Cultural Distances

> HYPOTHESIS 1a: Cultural distances between the cultural groups will affect their success sharing.

Consider the path p1 on Figure 7. According to the CALIS procedure (Table 35), the effect of differences in:
1. PDI on success sharing is significant for the Highlanders (at the 0.01 level);
2. MAS on success sharing is significant for:
    - The Coastalers (at the 0.10 level);
    - The Highlanders (at the 0.05 level);
3. TAS on success sharing is significant for the Merina (at the 0.10 level).

That is to say, HYPOTHESIS 1a can be **accepted**.

> HYPOTHESIS 1b: The effect of cultural distances on success sharing will not be the same for all of the cultural groups.

Also, consider path p1 (Table 35). One would remark that:
1. To the Coastalers, success sharing is positively and significantly affected by differences in PDI; whereas, it is significantly the opposite for the Highlanders;
2. Differences in TAS negatively and significantly affect success sharing in regard to the Merina only.

In other words, HYPOTHESIS 1b can be **accepted**.

> HYPOTHESIS 2a: Cultural distances between the cultural groups will affect their mental models sharing.

Consider path p2 on Figure 7. According to the CALIS

procedure (Table 35), the effect of differences in:
1. PDI on mental models sharing is significant for:
   - The Coastalers (at the 0.05 level);
   - The Merina (at the 0.01 level);
2. SPA on mental models sharing is significant for:
   - The Coastalers (at the 0.05 level);
   - The Highlanders (at the 0.05 level).

In brief, HYPOTHESIS 2a can be **accepted**.

HYPOTHESIS 2b: The effect of cultural distances on mental models sharing will not be the same for all of the cultural groups.

According to the CALIS procedure (Table 35), HYPOTHESIS 2b can be **accepted** because:
1. For the Coastalers, mental models sharing is negatively and significantly affected by differences in PDI; whereas it is significantly the opposite for the Merina;
2. For the Coastalers and the Highlanders, the effect of differences in SPA on mental models sharing is significantly positive, whereas for the Merina it is the opposite (though it is not significant).

HYPOTHESIS 3a: Cultural distances between the cultural groups will affect their vision sharing.

Concerning the path p3 (Figure 7), Table 35 shows that the effect of differences in:
1. PDI on mental models sharing is significant for the Highlanders;
2. MAS on mental models sharing is significant for the Merina;
3. TAS on mental models sharing is significant for the Coastalers.

In other words, HYPOTHESIS 3a can be **accepted**.

> HYPOTHESIS 3b: The effect of cultural distances on vision sharing will not be the same for all of the cultural groups.

According to the CALIS procedure (Table 35):
1. The Highlanders only view differences in PDI positively and significantly affecting vision sharing;
2. For the Merina only, differences in MAS significantly affect vision sharing;
3. The Coastalers only view differences in TAS significantly affecting vision sharing.

Therefore, HYPOTHESIS 3b can be **accepted**.

> HYPOTHESIS 4a: Cultural distances between the cultural groups will affect their core competence development.

Consider the path p4, as it is shown on Figure 7. The CALIS procedure (Table 35) says that the effect of differences in:
1. PDI on core competence development is significant for:
    - The Highlanders at the 0.10 level;
    - The Merina at the 0.05 level;
2. TAS on core competence development is significant for:
    - The Highlanders at the 0.01 level;
    - The Merina at the 0.10 level;
3. SPA on core competence development is significant for the Highlanders at the 0.10 level.

That is to say, HYPOTHESIS 4a can be **accepted**.

HYPOTHESIS 4b: The effect of cultural distances on core competence development will not be the same for all of the cultural groups.

According to Table 35 (consider the rows corresponding to the path p4):
1. The effects of differences in PDI on core competence development are significantly negative for the Highlanders, whereas they are significantly positive for the Merina;
2. Though the effect of differences in TAS on core competence development are positive to all of the cultural groups, they are not significant in regard to the Coastalers;
3. The effect of differences in SPA on core competence development is only significantly positive in regard to the Highlanders.

Hence, HYPOTHESIS 4b can be **accepted**.

5.4.4.2. Hypotheses on the Conditions for an Effective Multicultural Management

In order to make this book readable and to keep its volume reasonable, all the figures related to this section would not be presented. Nevertheless, these figures are available and can be provided anytime that they would be required.

Table 36: Summary of the REG procedure (STAR)

	Parameter estimates for:			
	Coastal	Highland	Merina	Together
Dep. Var.: Open and equal opport.				
Intercep	3.289135***	3.071077***	2.721864***	3.024140***
Training	-0.016786	-0.059086	0.201349**	0.050294
Job performance eval. feedback	0.091119	-1.098450*	0.133724	0.066521
Job performance eval. transparency	-0.051170	0.360628**	-0.144829	-0.054206
Dep. Var.: Success sharing				
Intercep	3.032938***	3.986486***	3.257444***	3.283223***
Open and equal opportunity	0.069170	-0.141892	0.178040	0.079963
Dep. Var.: Communication				
Intercep	11.903846***	14.328828***	14.498452***	13.810774***
Repeated interactions and soc. net.	0.464286***	0.244667	0.304334	0.328446***
Dep. Var.: Conflicts				
Intercep	13.411538***	10.178247***	12.771930***	12.305020***
Repeated interactions and soc. net.	0.003061	0.164097	0.071930	0.072076
Dep. Var.: Mutual understanding				
Intercep	3.250000***	3.661668***	2.632611***	3.286105***
Repeated interactions and soc. net.	0.025510	-0.017635	0.062023	0.017652
Dep. Var.: Mutual trust and respect				
Intercep	3.573077***	3.657867**	6.515996***	4.957638***
Repeated interactions and soc. net.	0.225510***	0.173178*	0.121878*	0.156224***
Dep. Var.: Cooperation				
Intercep	3.865385***	2.722070***	3.922601***	3.585515***
Repeated interactions and soc. net.	-0.015306	0.061668**	0.016718	0.016552
Dep. Var.: Mental models sharing				
Intercep	2.518842*	-1.244352	0.829641	1.064692
Communication	-0.005384	-0.078661*	-0.114711**	-0.071674**
Mutual understanding	0.730780**	0.445068**	1.254832***	0.816705***
Mutual trust and respect	-0.078004	0.209316**	-0.274383*	0.028702
Cooperation	-0.550140	0.636363**	0.420456	-0.068081
Dep. Var.: Vision sharing				
Intercep	2.878471***	2.401826***	0.990793**	2.126623***
Success sharing	0.167798	0.168950	0.689335***	0.354728***
Mental models sharing	-0.005765	0.100457	0.053588	0.044836
Dep. Var.: Higher-level learning				
Intercep	1.381227	2.315073**	-0.539864	0.931535
Vision sharing	1.150632***	0.689922**	2.019904***	1.316681***
Lower-level learning	0.173243	0.389937***	0.012245	0.193764**
Dep. Var.: Satisfaction				
Intercep	38.524814***	23.989071*	47.484466***	41.200034***
Higher-level learning	1.154748	3.598361**	-0.192899	0.814587
Dep. Var.: Improvement				
Intercep	24.805784***	26.845173***	22.114374***	23.646356***
Higher-level learning	-0.242673	-0.773224	0.162001	-0.123855
Dep. Var.: Willingness to co-succeed				
Intercep	30.657679***	30.648452***	28.577672***	30.135433***
Higher-level learning	0.282532	0.497268	0.464493*	0.374893**

t-test; *p<0.10 **p<0.05 ***p<0.01

Success Sharing.

> HYPOTHESIS 5: All employees from all cultural backgrounds will recognize that the more training they receive, the more open and equal their opportunity to succeed and be promoted will be.

According to the REG procedure (Table 36), the Coastalers and the Highlanders' seem not to confirm this hypothesis because, for these cultural groups, the parameter estimates of the independent variable "training" are negative.

According to Figures 42 and 43, however, though a fluctuation appears in the middle of each curve, the figures would confirm the hypothesis before and after the fluctuation. In other words, they would suggest that the more training the employees will get, the more open and equal their opportunity to succeed and be promoted will be, though a temporary turbulence may occur in the course of time.

Moreover, Table 36 and Figure 44 suggest that, when the sample employees are considered together:
- The parameter estimate for the sample employees is positive;
- The slope of the sample employees' curve is positive.

That is, HYPOTHESIS 5 could be **accepted**.

Figure 42: The relationship between training and equal opportunity to succeed and be promoted according to the Coastalers at STAR

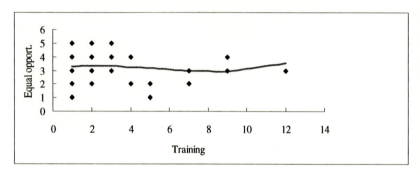

Figure 43: The relationship between training and equal opportunity to succeed and be promoted according to the Highlanders at STAR

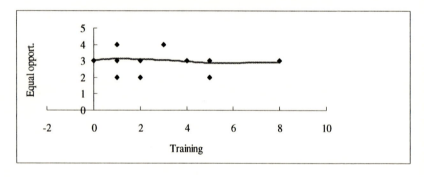

Figure 44: The relationship between training and equal opportunity to succeed and be promoted according to the sampled employees at STAR

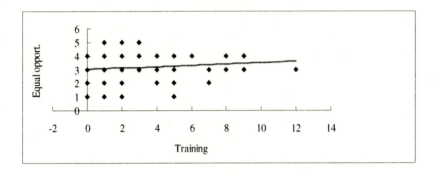

HYPOTHESIS 6: All employees from all cultural backgrounds will recognize that the more job performance evaluation feedback they receive, the more open and equal their opportunities to succeed and be promoted will be.

The output of the REG procedure (Table 36) suggests that the Highlanders do not confirm the hypothesis because, for this cultural group, the parameter estimates of the independent variable "feedback" is negative.

1. According to Figure 45, however, the slope of the first part of the curve is not negative;
2. When considered together without any categorization, the sampled employees appear to support the hypothesis. Indeed:
    - Table 36 shows that the parameter estimate for the sampled employees is positive;
    - Figure 46 presents a curve with a slightly positive slope.

Therefore, HYPOTHESIS 6 could be **discussed**.

Figure 45: The relationship between job performance evaluation and equal opportunity to succeed and be promoted according to the Highlanders at STAR

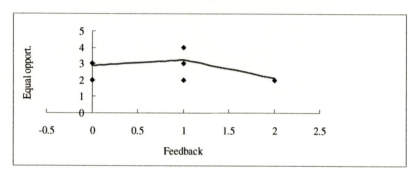

Figure 46: The relationship between job performance evaluation and equal opportunity to succeed and be promoted according to the sampled employees at STAR

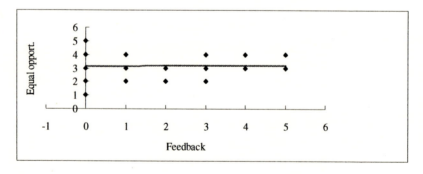

HYPOTHESIS 7: All employees from all cultural backgrounds will recognize that the more job performance evaluation is transparent, the more open and equal their opportunities to succeed and be promoted will be.

The output of the REG procedure (Table 36) indicates that the Coastalers and the Merina do not support this hypothesis since, for them, the parameter estimates of the independent "transparency" are negative.

However, HYPOTHESIS 7 could be **discussed** since:
- Figure 47 shows a curve with a slightly positive slope;
- Figure 48 indicates that the first part of the curve has a positive slope;
- Figure 49 indicates that though fluctuations appear at the beginning and at the middle of the curve, most parts of it show positive slopes.

Figure 47: The relationship between job performance evaluation transparency and equal opportunity to succeed and be promoted according to the Coastalers at STAR

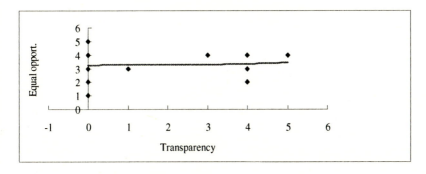

Figure 48: The relationship between job performance evaluation transparency and equal opportunity to succeed and be promoted according to the Merina at STAR

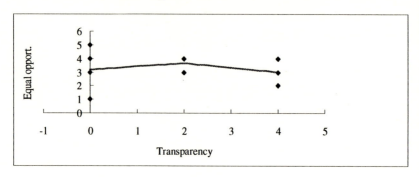

Figure 49: The relationship between job performance evaluation transparency and equal opportunity to succeed and be promoted according to the sampled employees at STAR

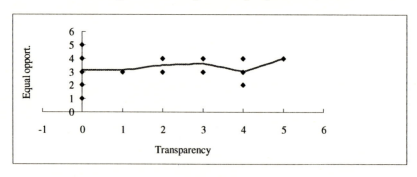

HYPOTHESIS 8: All employees from all cultural backgrounds will recognize that the more their opportunities to succeed and be promoted are open and equal, the more success sharing there will be.

According to the REG procedure (Table 36), the Highlanders appear not to confirm this hypothesis because the parameter estimates of the independent variable "open and equal opportunity" for this cultural group is negative.

Figures 50 and 51, however, seem to support the hypothesis since they present curves with positive slopes. In other words, based on the figures, HYPOTHESIS 8 could be **accepted**.

Figure 50: The relationship between equal opportunity to succeed and be promoted and success sharing according to the Highlanders at STAR

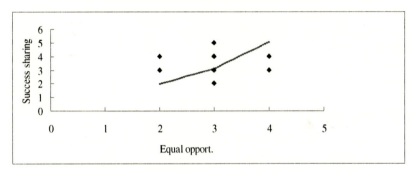

Figure 51: The relationship between equal opportunity to succeed and be promoted and success sharing according to the sampled employees at STAR

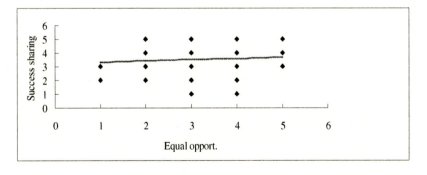

Mental Models Sharing.

> **HYPOTHESIS 9:** All employees from all cultural backgrounds will recognize that the more repeated interactions and social networks there are, the better their communication will be.

According to the REG procedure (Table 36), all the cultural groups confirm the hypothesis because the parameter estimates of the independent variable "repeated interactions and social networks" for all of the cultural groups are positive though not all of them are significant. That is, with the REG procedure, HYPOTHESIS 9 could be **accepted**.

> **HYPOTHESIS 10:** All employees from all cultural backgrounds will recognize that the more repeated interactions and social networks there are, the less conflicts there will be.

The output of the REG procedure (Table 36) indicates that all of the cultural groups' members do not support this hypothesis since the parameter estimates of the independent variable "repeated interactions and social networks" are positive for all of them.

However, according to Figures 52-55:
- None of the cultural groups appears to refuse the hypothesis flatly. Indeed, all the curves present fluctuations;
- The Highlanders' curve (Figure 53) suggests that the more repeated interactions and social networks there are, the less conflicts there will be though it may be difficult at the beginning. Indeed, the first part of the curve has a positive slope but the second part has a negative one.
- The sample employees partially support the hypothesis since the last parts of their curve (Figure 55) present positive slopes.

Therefore, with the figures, **HYPOTHESIS 10** could be **discussed**.

Figure 52: The relationship between repeated interactions and social networks and non-constructive conflicts according to the Coastalers at STAR

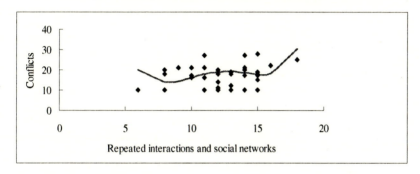

Figure 53: The relationship between repeated interactions and social networks and non-constructive conflicts according to the Highlanders at STAR

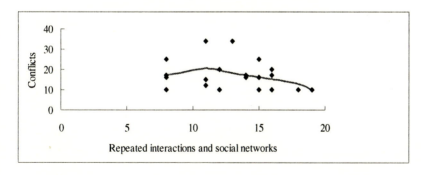

Figure 54: The relationship between repeated interactions and social networks and non-constructive conflicts according to the Merina at STAR

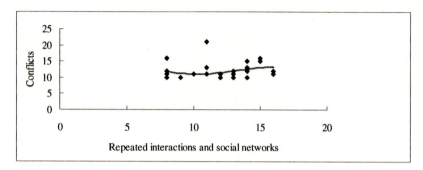

Figure 55: The relationship between repeated interactions and social networks and non-constructive conflicts according to the sampled employees at STAR

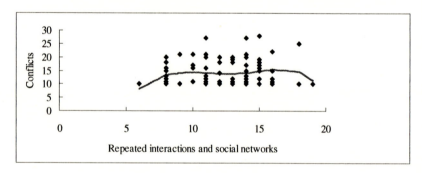

HYPOTHESIS 11: All employees from all cultural backgrounds will recognize that the more repeated interactions and social networks there are, the more they will understand each other.

The REG procedure (Table 36) suggests that the Highlanders appear not to support the hypothesis since the parameter estimates of the independent variable "repeated interactions and social networks" are negative for this cultural group.

However, considering:
- Figure 56, a part of the curve only (in the middle) has a negative slope;
- Figure 57, the curve has a slightly positive slope;
- Table 36, the parameter estimate of the independent variable "repeated interactions and social networks" is positive for the sampled employees considered together.

Thus, **HYPOTHESIS 11** could be **accepted**.

Figure 56: The relationship between repeated interactions and social networks and mutual understanding according to the Highlanders at STAR

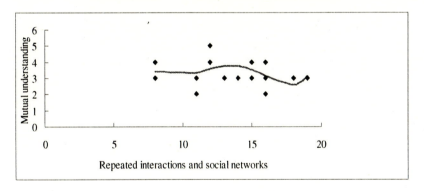

Figure 57: The relationship between repeated interactions and social networks and mutual understanding according to the sampled employees at STAR

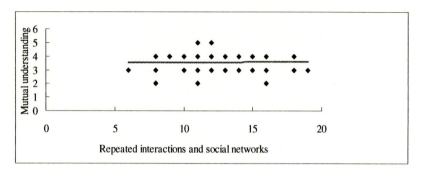

> HYPOTHESIS 12: All employees from all cultural backgrounds will recognize that the more repeated interactions and social networks there are, the more they will trust and respect each other.

The output of the REG procedure (Table 36) shows that all of the cultural groups significantly support the hypothesis. In other words, based upon the REG procedure, HYPOTHESIS 12 can be **accepted**.

> HYPOTHESIS 13: All employees from all cultural backgrounds will recognize that the more repeated interactions and social networks there are, the more cooperation there will be.

The output of the REG procedure (Table 36) shows that the Coastalers seem not to confirm the hypothesis because the parameter estimate of the independent variable is negative for this cultural group. However, considering:
- Figure 58, the second part of the curve has a positive slope, which supports the hypothesis;

- Figure 59, the curve has a positive slope;
- Table 36, the parameter estimate for the sample employees is positive.

In other words, **HYPOTHESIS 13** could be **accepted**.

Figure 58: The relationship between repeated interactions and social networks and cooperation according to the Coastalers at STAR

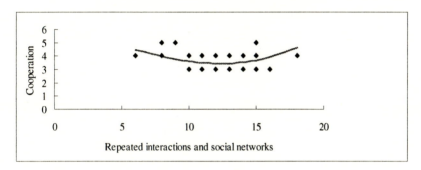

Figure 59: The relationship between repeated interactions and social networks and cooperation according to the sampled employees at STAR

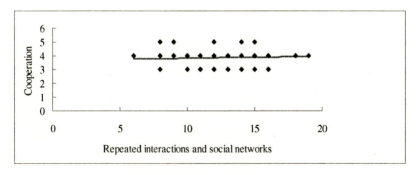

HYPOTHESIS 14: All employees from all cultural backgrounds will recognize that the better their communication is, the more mental models sharing there will be.

According to the REG procedure (Table 36), all of the cultural groups' members do not support the hypothesis because the parameter estimates of the independent variable "communication" are negative for all of them.

However, considering Figures 60-63, all of the curves have fluctuations. That is, none of the cultural groups appear to refuse the hypothesis flatly.

That is, HYPOTHESIS 14 could be **discussed**.

Figure 60: The relationship between quality of communication and mental models sharing according to the Coastalers at STAR

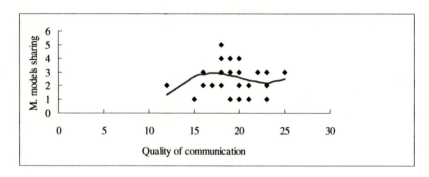

Figure 61: The relationship between quality of communication and mental models sharing according to the Highlanders

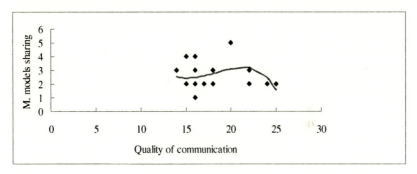

Figure 62: The relationship between quality of communication and mental models sharing according to the Merina at STAR

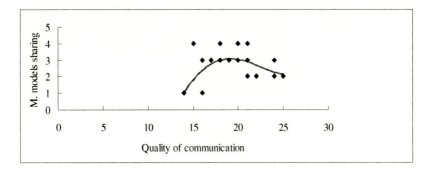

Figure 63: The relationship between quality of communication and mental models sharing according to the sampled employees

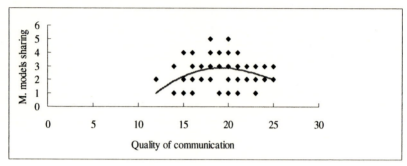

> **HYPOTHESIS 15:** All employees from all cultural backgrounds will recognize that the more they understand each other, the more mental models sharing there will be.

The output of the REG procedure (Table 36) shows that all of the cultural groups significantly support the hypothesis. In other words, HYPOTHESIS 15 can be **accepted.**

> **HYPOTHESIS 16:** All employees from all cultural backgrounds will recognize that the more they trust and respect each other, the more mental models sharing there will be.

- The REG procedure (Table 36) indicates that the Coastalers and the Merina appear not to support the hypothesis, yet when the sample employees are considered together, the parameter estimate of the independent variable "mutual trust and respect" is positive.
- Though Figure 64 appears to confirm the REG procedure's output, Figures 65 and 66 suggest that, the Merina and the sample employees considered together seem to support the

hypothesis.

In a word, **HYPOTHESIS 16** could also be **discussed**.

Figure 64: The relationship between mutual trust and respect and mental models sharing according to the Coastalers at STAR

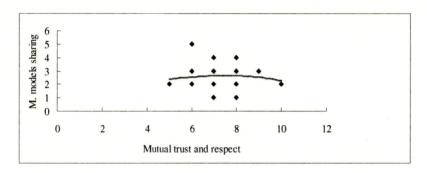

Figure 65: The relationship between mutual trust and respect and mental models sharing according to the Merina at STAR

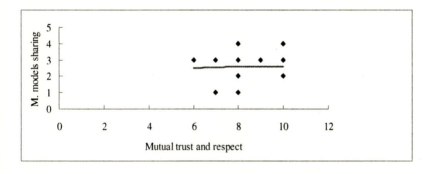

Figure 66: The relationship between mutual trust and respect and mental models sharing according to the sampled employees

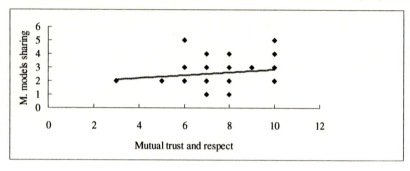

HYPOTHESIS 17: All employees from all cultural backgrounds will recognize that the more they cooperate, the more mental models sharing there will be.

Table 36 indicates that the Coastalers seem not to support the hypothesis because the parameter estimate of the independent variable is negative for this cultural group.

Though Figure 67 appears to be consistent with the output of the REG procedure, Figure 68 shows a curve with a positive slope. Therefore, HYPOTHESIS 17 could be **discussed**.

Figure 67: The relationship between cooperation
and mental models sharing
according to the Coastalers at STAR

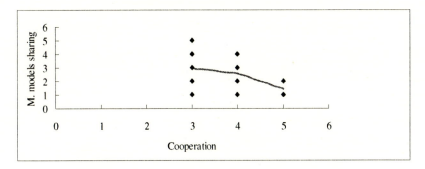

Figure 68: The relationship between cooperation
and mental models sharing
according to the sampled employees at STAR

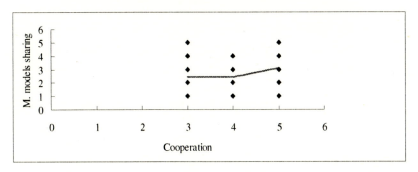

Vision Sharing.

> HYPOTHESIS 18: All employees from all cultural backgrounds will recognize that the more success sharing there is, the more vision sharing there will be.

Consider the path p5 on Figure 7. The output of the CALIS procedure (Table 35) shows that, considering the cultural groups' differences in PDI, MAS, TAS, and SPA, all of the cultural groups seem to support the hypothesis, though the standardized coefficients are not significant.

Also, the output of the REG procedure (Table 36) indicates that the parameter estimates of the independent variable are positive for all of the cultural groups.

That is, HYPOTHESIS 18 could be **accepted**.

> HYPOTHESIS 19: All employees from all cultural backgrounds will recognize that the more mental models sharing there is, the more vision sharing there will be.

Considering the path p6, in regard to the cultural groups' differences in PDI, MAS, and SPA, the CALIS procedure's output (Table 35) shows that, the Coastalers do not confirm the hypothesis.

The output of the REG procedure (Table 36) confirms this result because the parameter estimate of the independent variable is negative for the Coastalers.

However, considering:
- Figure 69, the second part of the curve has a positive slope;
- Figure 70, the slope of the curve is positive;
- The last column of Table 36, the parameter estimate of the independent variable is positive for the sample employees considered together.

In other words, **HYPOTHESIS 19** could be **accepted**.

Figure 69: The relationship between mental models sharing
and vision sharing
according to the Coastalers at STAR

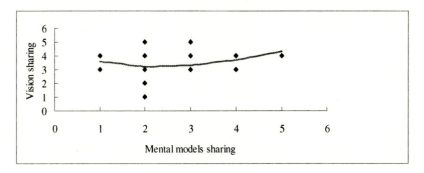

Figure 70: The relationship between mental models sharing
and vision sharing
according to the sampled employees at STAR

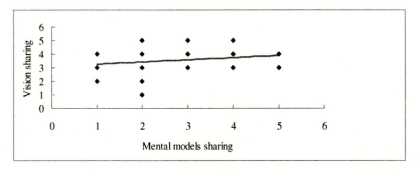

Core Competence Development.

> HYPOTHESIS 20: All employees from all cultural backgrounds will recognize that the more vision sharing there is, the more core competence development there will be.

Concerning the path p7 (Figure 7), the output of the CALIS procedure (Table 35) shows that, in regard to all cultural dimensions, all of the cultural groups appear to support the hypothesis.

The output of the REG procedure (Table 36) confirms the CALIS procedure's result by showing significantly a positive parameter estimate of the independent variable "core competence development" for all of the cultural groups.

Thus, based upon the REG procedure, HYPOTHESIS 20 can be **accepted**.

> HYPOTHESIS 21: All employees from all cultural backgrounds will recognize that their higher-level learning is directly related to their lower-level learning success.

According to the output of the REG procedure (Table 36), all of the cultural groups seem to support the hypothesis because the parameter estimates of the independent variables are positive for all of them (though not all of them are significant). That is, considering the REG procedure, HYPOTHESIS 21 could be **accepted**.

5.4.4.3. Hypotheses on the Linkage Between Core Competence Development and Performance

> HYPOTHESIS 22: All employees from all cultural backgrounds will recognize that the more they develop their core competence, the more satisfaction they will have.

Consider path p8 on Figure 7. According to the the CALIS procedure (Table 35):
1. In regard to differences in PDI and SPA, the Coastalers appear not to support the hypothesis;
2. In regard to differences in MAS, the Highlanders seem not to confirm the hypothesis.

In addition, with the REG procedure (Table 36), the Merina appear not to support the hypothesis because the parameter estimate of the independent variable is negative for this cultural group.

However, if one consider:
- Figure 71, the first part of the curve has a positive slope;
- Figure 72, the slope of the curve is positive. This is consistent with the last column of Table 36 which shows a positive parameter estimate of the independent variable for the sample employees considered together;
- The output of the CALIS procedure (Table 35), in regard of differences in TAS, all of the cultural group significantly confirm the hypothesis.

That is, HYPOTHESIS 22 could be **discussed**.

Figure 71: The relationship between core competence development and satisfaction according to the Merina at STAR

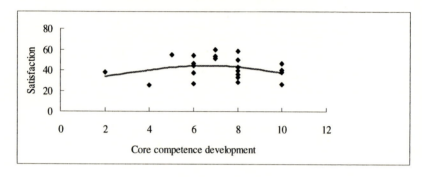

Figure 72: The relationship between core competence development and satisfaction according to the sampled employees at STAR

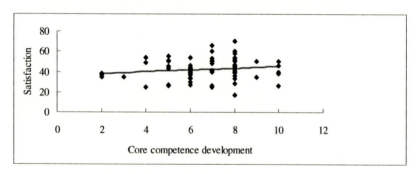

HYPOTHESIS 23: All employees from all cultural backgrounds will recognize that the more they develop their core competence, the more improvement there will be.

Concerning the path p9 on Figure 7, the output of the CALIS procedure (Table 35) suggests that:

1. In regard to differences in PDI, MAS, and SPA, the Coastalers appear not to confirm the hypothesis;
2. In regard to differences in PDI and TAS, the Highlanders seem not to support the hypothesis;
3. In regard to differences in MAS and SPA, the Merina appear not to confirm the hypothesis.

The output of the REG procedure (Table 36) also indicates that the parameter estimates of the independent variable "core competence development" are negative for the Coastalers and the Highlanders.

However, considering Figures 73-75, the last part of the curves of these figures have positive slopes though fluctuations appear at the beginning or in the middle of them. That is to say, the cultural groups' members recognize that the more they develop their core competence, the more improvement there will be, though difficulty may appear at the beginning or in the course of the core competence development.

In other words, based upon the figures, HYPOTHESIS 23 could be **accepted**.

Figure 73: The relationship between core competence development and improvement according to the Coastalers at STAR

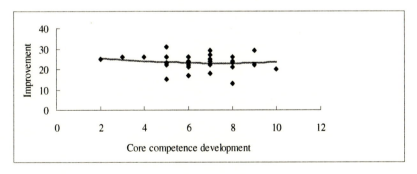

Figure 74: The relationship between core competence development and improvement according to the Highlanders at STAR

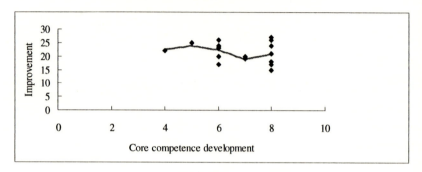

Figure 75: The relationship between core competence development and improvement according to the sampled employees at STAR

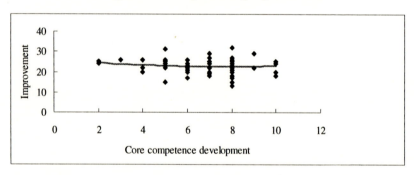

> HYPOTHESIS 24: All employees from all cultural backgrounds will recognize that the more they develop their core competence, the more they will be willing to co-succeed.

Considering the path p10 on Figure 7, the output of the CALIS procedure (Table 35) suggests that, the standardized

coefficients for:
1. The Coastalers are negative in regard to differences in PDI and SPA;
2. The Highlanders are negative in regard to differences in TAS and SPA;
3. The Merina are negative in regard to differences in MAS, TAS, and SPA.

The output of the REG procedure (Table 36) however suggests that all of the cultural groups seem to support the hypothesis since the parameter estimates of the independent variable are positive (though not significant) for all of them.
That is, with the REG procedure, **HYPOTHESIS 24** could be **accepted**.

5.4.5. Interpretations, Findings, and Discussions

The specific results of the hypotheses testing are as follows:

1. Like with KRAOMA's case, as it was expected, all the hypotheses concerning the effects of cultural distances on success sharing, mental models sharing, vision sharing, and core competence development have been accepted. In other words, the Coastalers, the Highlanders, and the Merina's cultural distances do really matter at STAR, so that they have to be carefully considered.
Here also, the result supports the statement that cultural diversity does influence management practices and its impacts can be identified in the motivational, the interaction, the visioning, and the learning processes.

2. Furthermore, the results show that the effects of cultural distances on success sharing, mental models sharing, vision sharing, and core competence development are not the same for all of the cultural groups. This indicates that when the different cultural groups interact in the workplace some of them would likely be found *more negatively* affected by the differences in a given specific dimension of culture content (PDI or MAS or TAS or SPA). And, thereby, they would likely impede the integration and combination of the employees' ideas and competencies, attitudes and behaviors, ways of thinking and doing ...

Table 37 shows that, regarding the effect of:
- Differences in PDI and MAS on success sharing, the Highlanders would be found to be the most negatively affected;
- Differences in TAS on success sharing, the Merina would be found to be the most negatively affected;
- Differences in PDI on mental models sharing, the Coastalers would be identified to be the most negatively affected;
- Differences in TAS on vision sharing, the Coastalers would be found to be the most negatively affected;
- Differences in PDI on core competence development, the Highlanders would be identified to be the most negatively affected.

Table 37: The most negatively affected cultural groups in regard to differences in PDI, MAS, TAS, and SPA (STAR)

Concerning	MOSTLY affected cultural groups	By differences in:			
		PDI	MAS	TAS	SPA
Success sharing	Highland	X	X		
	Merina			X	
Mental Models sharing	Coastal	X			
Vision sharing	Coastal			X	
Higher-level learning	Highland	X			

3. According to Table 38, the Coastalers and the Merina appear to be the two antagonistic cultural groups, whereas the Highlanders seem to hold a strategic cultural position between them.

Table 38: The cultural groups' cultural positions (STAR)

Cultural Dimensions	Positions
Power Distance Index	Coastal > *Highland* > Merina (0.29) (0.03) (-0.30)
Masculinity Orientation	Coastal > *Highland* > Merina (0.19) (0.17) (-0.30)
Task Orientation	Coastal > Merina > Highland (0.28) (0.09) (-0.27)
Space Orientation	Coastal > *Highland* > Merina (0.19) (0.08) (-0.26)

* (Standardized mean)

Therefore, as it has been stated for KRAOMA, it might be possible that the Highlanders would have:
- Intermediate and impartial attitudes, behaviors, way of thinking, way of doing ...
- The potential to:
  - ➤ Play the role of cultural and functional interface;
  - ➤ Be the promoter of multicultural learning at STAR.

4. According to Table 39:
- Power/dominance discrepancies exist between the cultural groups;
- The Merina (dominant group) hold advantages in power/dominance and economic resource.

Table 39: The cultural groups' power/dominance positions (STAR)

Power/Dominance	Positions
Occupational Position	Merina > Coastal, *Highland* (1.62) (1.33)
Wage	Merina > Coastal > *Highland* (11.11) (8.62) (7.93)
Educational Level	Merina > Highland > Coastal (3.84) (3.48) (3.31)

* (Standardized mean)

As it has been mentioned in KRAOMA's case, regarding the power/dominance discrepancies and the satisfaction levels of the Coastalers and the Highlanders (Table 40), it seems that:

1. The Highlanders feel less dissatisfied than their counterparts Coastalers and prefer to be content with the status quo. Indeed, their power/dominance position appears not to allow them to enter in a contest and conquer the highest position. This is what one would call *a feeling of resignation.*

2. On the contrary, the Coastalers feel more discomfort because their current power/dominance position seems to allow them to hope and contend for a better/higher position (that is why they cry out for an open and equal opportunity). This is what one would name *a feeling of challenge.*

3. The Merina are the most satisfied group because they hold the highest power/dominance position and, hypothetically,

Table 40: The cultural groups' satisfaction levels (STAR)

Cultural Groups	Satisfaction Levels
Merina Group	48.78
Highland Group	*46.11*
Coastal Group	45.90

* Each group: 17 items
* 1 item: Not at all (1) - Very satisfied (5)

the more a group holds the power, the more this group is satisfied. They have what one would describe as *a feeling of contentment*.

Here, the Highlanders' feeling confirms the above-mentioned view of this group's potentiality to play the cultural and functional interfaces' roles. Indeed, since they seem to accept to resign the race for higher power/dominance positions, they would likely put themselves out of any potential unlearning situation (e.g., due to dispute or destructive conflict). And, thereby, incite a more flexible and dynamic climate (e.g., favored by constructive conflict), which would welcome multicultural learning.

Nevertheless, Cox (1993) asserts that if power/dominance discrepancies/imbalances persist too long, then they may have the effect of reducing the motivation and the perceived opportunity among members of non-dominant groups to participate and to excel in their fullest potential in diverse-group setting. Hence, the importance of seeking more balanced representation and power among the cultural groups.

5. **HYPOTHESIS 6** has not been accepted because the slope of the second part of the curve for the Highlanders was negative. Since however, the sample employees as a whole appear to support the hypothesis, this would not reject the potential contribution of job performance evaluation feedback in enhancing an open and equal opportunity to succeed and be promoted. It would rather confirm the need of job performance evaluation feedback in a multicultural workplace.

6. In the same way, **HYPOTHESIS 7** and **HYPOTHESIS 10** could be subject of discussions since the related curves present fluctuations. However:
- Since the last part of the curve of Figure 49 has positive

slopes, this would rather indicate that the cultural groups' members would support **HYPOTHESIS 7** when they are together, though it might not smooth out at the beginning.
- Concerning **HYPOTHESIS 10**, it could be fair to say that the sampled employees considered without any cultural categorization would support the hypothesis, since:
  - ➢ Fluctuations appear in the curves of Figures 52-55. Indeed, this would mean that none of the cultural groups seem to flatly reject the hypothesis;
  - ➢ The last part of the curve of Figure 55 (related to the sampled employees) presents positive slope.

7. HYPOTHESIS 14 has been said to be subject of discussion because the last parts of the curves of Figures 61-63 present negative slopes. Similarly to **KRAOMA**'s case, this result:
- Seems to hint the existence of hostility between the cultural groups' members. Indeed, beyond the historical background of the island:
  - ✓ Many of their viewpoints are significantly opposite from each other (Table 36);
  - ✓ As mentioned earlier, the cultural groups' cultures, power/dominance positions, satisfaction levels, and feelings toward the status quo are different from each other (Tables 38-40).
- Is congruent with Figure 76 which shows that difference in cultural group (regional origin) is the major source of conflict at STAR (total score = 90). On average, all of the sample employees affirm that conflicts due to cultural group differences happen in the firm, at least, rarely. Figure 77 indicates that, among the 70 employees in the sample (67.96%) who assert this fact:
  - ✓ 36 employees (51.43%) state that conflicts occur rarely;
  - ✓ 30 employees (42.86%) affirm that conflicts happen

occasionally;
- ✓ 4 employees (5.71%) declare that conflicts are frequent.

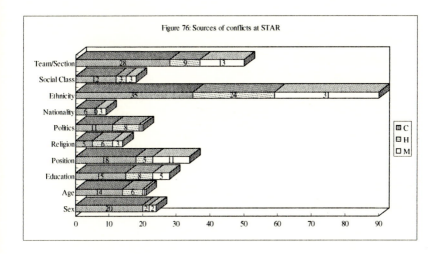

Figure 76: Sources of conflicts at STAR

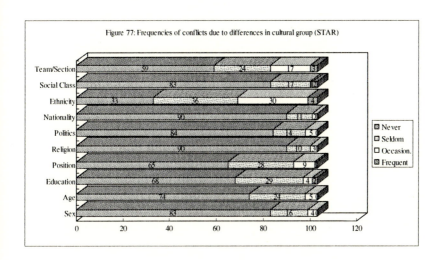

Figure 77: Frequencies of conflicts due to differences in cultural group (STAR)

8. Though HYPOTHESIS 16 and HYPOTHESIS 17 have not been accepted (because the Coastalers do not agree that more mutual trust and respect and more cooperation would lead to more mental models sharing), they can be subject of discussions because when considered together, the sampled employees support the hypotheses.

Indeed, apparently, these results seem to indicate that, though the Coastalers' viewpoint appears to be pessimistic, their point of view is rather weakened or even shifted when they are together with the other cultural groups who support the hypotheses. This suggests that the presence and interactions of culturally diverse workforce at the workplace could bring contextual change and dynamism among the cultural groups. As a result, everybody would not likely be stuck with his/her own ideas, viewpoints, ways of thinking, and so on.

9. HYPOTHESIS 22 also can be subject of discussion because, though the slope of the Merina's curve (Figure 71) is only positive to some degree of core competence development:
- The result does not suggest that the Merina group members entirely disagree with the hypothesis;
- The CALIS procedure suggests that, in regard of differences in TAS, all of the cultural group significantly support the hypothesis;
- Figure 72 indicates that, when considered together, the sample employees support the hypothesis.

If the third reason could just be interpreted as a change or a shift in the Merina's viewpoint when they are together with the other cultural groups, then, with point **7.**, one could maybe deduce that:
1. The conceptual model is suitable for a multicultural workforce;
2. HYPOTHESES 6, 7, 10, 14, 16, 17 and 22 could be accepted at the multicultural level.

10. Table 41 summarizes the result of the hypotheses testing.

Table 41: Result of the hypotheses testing with STAR's data

Hypotheses on:	Accepted	Discussed	Rejected	Total
1. Effects of Cultural Distances	8			8
2. The Conditions for an Effective Multicultural Management	11	6		17
3. The Linkage between Core Competence and Performance	2	1		3
TOTAL	21	7	0	28

Similarly to KRAOMA's case, though the feature of the result appears to suggest the consistency and the suitability of the framework, here, it would be argued that, if the Highlanders would contribute and efficiently play the role of cultural and functional interfaces:
1. This framework would smooth out;
2. Multicultural workforce's balance would be reached;
3. STAR's situation could be ameliorated/improved.
4.

5.5. Summary: A Comparison of the Two Studied Companies

5.5.1. Similarities

The results of the hypotheses testing suggest that:

1. As it was expected, all the hypotheses concerning the effects of cultural distances on success sharing, mental models sharing, vision sharing, and core competence development have been accepted. In other words, the Coastalers, the Highlanders, and the Merina's cultural distances do really matter at KRAOMA and STAR, so that they have to be carefully considered.

2. Furthermore, the results show that the effects of cultural distances on success sharing, mental models sharing, vision sharing, and core competence development are not the same for all of the cultural groups. This indicates that when the different cultural groups interact in the workplace some of them would likely be found *more negatively* affected by the differences in a given specific dimension of culture content (PDI or MAS or TAS or SPA). And, thereby, they would likely impede the integration and combination of the employees' ideas and competencies, attitudes and behaviors, ways of thinking and doing ...

3. In both companies, the Coastalers and the Merina appear to be the two antagonistic cultural groups, whereas the Highlanders seem to hold a strategic cultural position between them. It might therefore be possible that the Highlanders would have:
- Intermediate and impartial attitudes, behaviors, way of thinking, way of doing ...;
- The potential to:
    - Play the role of cultural and functional interface;
    - Be the promoter of core competence development through multicultural learning at KRAOMA and STAR.

4. In both companies:
- Power/dominance discrepancies exist between the cultural groups;
- The Merina (dominant group) hold advantages in power/dominance and economic resource.

And regarding the power/dominance discrepancies and the satisfaction levels of the cultural groups, it seems that:

1. The Highlanders have what is called *a feeling of resignation*.
2. The Coastalers have what is named *a feeling of challenge*.
3. The Merina have what is described as *a feeling of contentment*.

The Highlanders' feeling confirms the view of this group members' potentiality to play the roles of cultural and functional interfaces. Indeed, since they seem to accept to resign the race for higher power/dominance positions, they would likely put themselves out of any potential unlearning situation (e.g., due to dispute or destructive conflict). And, thereby, they would incite a more flexible and dynamic climate (e.g., favored by constructive conflict), which would welcome core competence development through multicultural learning.

5. The results related to both companies seem to indicate:
- The existence of hostility between the cultural groups' members.
- That difference in cultural group (regional origin) is the major source of conflict at KRAOMA and STAR.

In other words, in both companies, the Highlanders appear not to play the role of cultural and functional interfaces.

6. Though some of the cultural groups sometimes appear to not support the hypotheses, their points of view are rather weakened or even shifted when they are together with the other cultural groups who support the hypotheses. This suggests that the presence and interactions of culturally diverse workforce at the workplace could bring contextual change and dynamism among the cultural groups. As a result, everybody would not likely be stuck with his/her own ideas, viewpoints, and ways of thinking...

7. In both cases, though the feature of the result appears to suggest the consistency and the suitability of the framework, it would be worthy to stress that, if a Third group[26] like the Highlanders would contribute to play the role of cultural and functional interfaces:
1. This framework would smooth out in both companies and, why not, in any multicultural organizations;
2. Multicultural workforce's balance would be easily reached;
3. Multicultural learning would be fostered and tapped;
4. Core competence would be developed and the status quo would be ameliorated and improved;
5. Competitive advantages would be sustained.

5.5.2. Differences

Though impressive similarities appear to exist between the two studied companies, some relevant differences are also worthy of comments:
1. First of all, though both companies hold multicultural workforce:
- The trends of the two companies' annual results seem to be different (Figures 10 and 12);
- The average satisfaction levels of the two companies' sampled employees are not the same (Table 42);
- The average viewpoints of the sampled employees concerning improved areas in their companies are different (Table 42);
- The average willingness of the two companies' sampled

---

[26] In this study, the *Third group* would be the group that is culturally intermediate but independent from the existing antagonistic groups. Because of their characteristics, the Third group members are assumed to be able to play the role of the cultural and the functional interfaces and to ease and foster the multicultural learning, thus, the core competence development in/of multicultural organizations.

employees to co-succeed are not the same (Table 42).

In sum, from these figures and tables, one could fairly say that STAR appears to have a better performance than KRAOMA, though both companies' performances are not good.

Table 42: Satisfaction levels, viewpoints about improveed areas, and willingness to co-succeed

	KRAOMA	STAR
Satisfaction levels	19.85	46.73
Improved areas	15.11	22.81
Willingness to co-succeed	32.41	32.68

2. Indeed, according to the result of the questionnaire for the management, STAR's management seems to be more aware about cultural diversity and multicultural management than KRAOMA's management does:
1. STAR educates its employees about cultural diversity whereas KRAOMA does not. KRAOMA's management rather thinks that it may hurt their employees' susceptibility;
2. Though all teams in both companies are fixed and multicultural, STAR's management did organize them purposefully because they did observe by experience that multicultural teams are more efficient than culturally homogeneous ones;
3. STAR's strategy to make each and all teams harmonized and effective rather appears to have the potentiality to foster multicultural learning than that of KRAOMA. In other words, at STAR, the management urges the members to communicate and to exchange their various viewpoints, whereas at KRAOMA, the management's strategy seems to be similar with the concept of salad bowl.

Moreover, Figures 40, 41, 76, and 77 suggest that the frequencies of conflicts at STAR are lower that those at KRAOMA.

3. In addition, STAR appears to have a better performance than KRAOMA because core competence development through multicultural learning at STAR seems to sparkle more than that at KRAOMA (Table 43).

Table 43: Core competence development at the two companies

	(Means)	
	KRAOMA	STAR
Learning opportunity at work	2.45	2.57
Step 1: **Core competence searching/acquisition**		
Training helpfulness	2.50	2.91
Volume of things learned	3.84	4.16
Step 2: **Selection and adaptation**		
Involvement of responsibles	2.89	3.60
Step 3: **Experimentation**		
Improvement	2.37	2.86
Step 4: **Core competence sharing**		
Occurence	3.16	3.40
Step 5: **Core competence development or co-creation of new core competence**		
Occurence	3.25	3.39

Number of levels: 5

Though, the difference appears to be insignificant in absolute value, this small difference has been found to have a considerable influence on the aforementioned organizations' performances. Indeed, the hypotheses related to the relation between core competence development and the organizations' performances have been mostly accepted.

Chapter 6
CASE ANALYSIS: THE CASE OF ERICSSON TOSHIBA

Though within recent years, managing cultural diversity has become a popular topic within management in general and organizational behavior and human resource management in particular, considerable confusion still exists on how multicultural organizations can effectively learn and how they can develop their core competence. Now, more than ever before, scholars and practitioners should move forward with the further idea of how to develop core competence through multicultural learning. To better pursue the discussions, this book addresses also the study with the real case of **Ericsson Toshiba Telecommunication Systems K.K.**

6.1. The Firm's Outline

Ericsson Toshiba Telecommunication Systems K.K. (shortened Ericsson Toshiba) is a joint venture company of Telefonaktiebolaget LM Ericsson (shortened Ericsson)—a world leader in cellular systems and in digital mobile communications—and Toshiba Corporation (shortened Toshiba)—a world leader in semi-conductor, information, and communications business field—established on September 1, 1992.

Ericsson Toshiba is headquartered in Shin-Yokohama and is owned 60 percent by Ericsson and 40 percent by Toshiba. Using equipment designed and manufactured by Ericsson, the company provides a full range of services, including the supply, installation, coordination, installation planning/management, maintenance, and other incidental operations for the mobile communication systems to be delivered to the Digital Phone

Group. This later is an inter-related group of Japanese regional cellular telephone service companies in which Toshiba is shareholder. In other words, the new company serves to link the partners to the Digital Phone Group. The alliance between Ericsson and Toshiba enhances telecommunication technologies in Japan and assists Ericsson's entrance into the Japanese market.

6.2. The Firm's Workforce

Table 44: Ericsson Toshiba's personnel data (December 31, 1995)

	Employees	
Country	**Number**	**%**
Japanese Group:	152	57.36
Japanese	152	
Scandinavian Group:	92	34.72
Denmark	9	
Finland	5	
Norway	2	
Sweden	76	
Third Group:	21	7.92
Australia	6	
Belgium	1	
Brazil	1	
Canada	1	
China	3	
Indonesia	1	
Ireland	2	
Mexico	2	
Singapore	1	
U.K.	1	
U.S.A.	2	
Total	**265**	**100.00**

Ericsson Toshiba's workforce consists of employees from 16

different countries who can be categorized into 3 groups (see Table 44):
1. The **Japanese group** (57%);
2. The **Scandinavian group** dominated by the Swedish (35%);
3. The **Third group** composed by the employees from other nationalities (8%).

6.3. The Firm's Core Competence

Ericsson Toshiba's main activity is concerned with personal digital cellular communication system. However:
- Since the firm's technical resources are mostly in Sweden and since Ericsson Toshiba does not yet have all the required technical proficiencies to run the business by itself[27], the firm still needs the Scandinavian expatriates' assistance to provide *the technical core competence*[28];
- Since the market is in Japan, obviously, a person who knows Japanese, Japanese culture, and Japanese way of doing business—that is, a person who holds *the commercial core competence*, is going to do this much better for the customers. Here then, it might be fair to say that no one else could be in a better position than the Japanese.

In brief, to effectively run the business, the Japanese need the Scandinavians for their technical core competence and the Scandinavians need the Japanese for their commercial core competence. *But why are the Third group members needed and hired?* Here is the concern of this study's argument.

---

[27] Ericsson Toshiba had just been experiencing its third winter.
[28] Usually, the expatriates are sent to Japan under 2 or 3-year contracts.

6.4. The Third Group's Strategic Functions

First of all, beyond the Japanese's lack in technical core competence and the Scandinavians' lack in commercial core competence, these two dominant groups' cultural distances seem to be significantly different (Hofstede, 1980). Consequently, they need some kind of cultural and functional interfaces to smooth their interactions and their core competence sharing/development[29]. Ericsson Toshiba, therefore, recruited the Third group members to play these functions because:

1. Most of these locally hired foreigners have Japanese ability and a fair knowledge of the Japanese culture and the Japanese way of doing business since they have been in Japan for many years (studying in Japanese universities and working in Japanese companies).

2. According to Table 45, the Third group members seem to hold an intermediate characteristic[30]. Therefore, they might have impartiality to the Japanese and to the Scandinavian groups. That is to say, they could have the ability to objectively enhance team members' mutual understanding and play the role of cultural and functional interfaces.

---

[29] Few of the Japanese, for example, are comfortable with English and none of the Scandinavians speak Japanese.
[30] Possibly because:
    1. Most of them understand (do not understand) and agree (disagree) on some of the two dominant groups'cultures, thus, some of their behavior and attitudes;
    2. By experience, most of them feel/realize/recognize that an intermediate characteristic is more efficient and more effective than those of the two dominant group members.

Table 45: Examples of employees' behaviors or desired behaviors at work

Indicators	Japanese Group Member	Scandinavian Group Member	Third Group Member
1. Emphasis	Group harmony, quality control, planning, and process	Time, output, and improvisation	Output, time, communication, and cooperation
2. Monitoring and Control	Very close	Not close	Close
3. Instructions	Too much detailed	Very short and very general	With few details
4. Problem Solving	By reporting to the manager or headquarter	Self resolution	Combination of two
5. Decision Making	In group	Individually	In group and then individually when common solution cannot be reached

A) The Scandinavians' emphases, monitoring style, instructions, problem solving and decision making are contradicting with those of the Japanese. That is why, conflict frequency between these two dominant groups is higher than that between each of them and the members of the Third group. This statement is also supported by the following remarks.

B) Scandinavians and members of the Third group are both stressing time and output. In other words, when considering these points, members of the Third group are rather closer to the Scandinavians than to their Japanese counterparts.

C) The emphases of the Third group's members on

communication and cooperation are congruent with Japanese's emphasis on group harmony. In other words, regarding this indicator, the Third group's members are in accord with the Japanese rather than with the Scandinavians.
D) The Third group's members monitoring style and control and instructions are more or less intermediate compared to those of the two dominant groups.
E) Problem solving and decision making strategies of the Third group's members are simply the combination of those of the Japanese and the Scandinavian groups.

3. Though the Third group's members are basically viewed as a minority in the workplace, their presence in a team could also make very stimulating and dynamic problem solving and decision making. Usually, for example, interviewees recognize that when only two cultures are attending a brainstorming meeting to solve problems or to make decisions, the participants tend to side with their own group and little is solved/decided. They have therefore found it easier to solve problems or to make decisions in a team having more than two cultures. Indeed, when more than two cultures are present, ideas and/or opinions and/or solutions and/or conclusions that are not purely Scandinavian or purely Japanese could often be co-created. The interviewees assert that, many times, difficult issues such as delays in deliveries and errors or broken materials are *only* sorted out through this approach.

4. From the same perspective, core competence development could also be facilitated in the presence of the Third group at the workplace. Indeed, the Scandinavians, for example, prefer the use of e-mail when giving/getting the feedback of their works and/or sharing information because it is quick and reduces the number of group meetings (indirect, immediate, and

Case Analysis: The Case of ERICSSON TOSHIBA

informal core competence sharing). Whereas, the Third group members would rather prefer to have a brainstorming meeting (even at the very workplace since the office organization allows it) to combine everybody's competencies and to develop the existing core competence (direct, immediate, and semi-formal core competence sharing). As one may notice, the Third group members' preferred strategy is closer to the Japanese OJT system than the Scandinavian approach, so that the Japanese might likely be more comfortable with them in terms of competence sharing. Moreover, spontaneous question/answer communication could be easily and effectively generated with the Third group members' strategy.

5. If the presence of the Third group members could ease and speed the transfer of the technical core competence, this could imply that their presence also could facilitate the attainment of the firm's vision, called *"Japanization"*, which is imperative for two reasons:
1. *In dealing with the customers:* obviously, a person who knows Japanese and Japanese way of doing business, is going to do this much better for the customers.
2. *In terms of expenses:* having expatriates on a contract in Japan is necessary at the beginning, but it is expensive.

Although the interests and the perspectives of the three cultural groups' members are various, almost all of them agree on this vision and hold themselves responsible toward it, both as individuals and as teams.
- The Japanese employees are working hard to be able to master as soon as possible the imported technical competence, so that they can:
  - ➢ Replace (technically) the existing expatriates;
  - ➢ Train the new recruits;
  - ➢ Become themselves expatriates when it will be

needed.
- The Scandinavians are doing their best in transferring the knowledge/core competence, so that they can:
  - Go back to their own country with the satisfaction that they have successfully fulfilled their contracts. It is worthy to note that this vision is common for all countries where Ericsson is operating. It always starts with a lot of experts, then they hired local employees that the experts trained for years and, after that, they run by themselves;
  - Get a new contract for another country, thus, a new challenge and a new experience.
- The locally hired foreigners in the Third group are working hard to affirm/signal their competencies, so that they can:
  - Be appointed to a higher level of responsibility;
  - Have the chance to be identified by Ericsson and hired by them later.

This is consistent with the fact that, when it started, Ericsson Toshiba was 80% foreigners and 20% Japanese. It was heavily foreigner but, now, it is partly going to switch to the opposite.

In sum, since Ericsson Toshiba's technical resources are mostly in Sweden and since the market is in Japan, one could fairly deduce that the company's culturally diverse workforce is not a choice but a necessity. Ericsson Toshiba therefore chose to have a balanced multicultural workforce—the two contradicting dominant groups are integrated with a minority group which can perform (1) an intermediate and combining approach and (2) a role of cultural and functional interfaces—so that it would be able to foster a multicultural learning. Not surprisingly, because of the cultural and functional interfaces:
- The Japanese declared that, beyond the technical matters, they have also learned, for example, Scandinavians' way of solving problems by improvisation.
- The Scandinavians stated that they have also learned, for

example, their Japanese counterparts' quality control strategy.
- The Third group's members said that, beyond the technical matters and the quality control, they have also learned, for example, Japanese way of harmonizing team (planning and process).

Since cultural diversity is "natural" sources of requisite variety—which is a condition for organizational learning (Teramoto et al., 1993a), both managerial and individual learning are crucial elements for successfully managing multicultural organizations (Rijamampianina, 1996b, 1996c).

6.5. The New Concept of Contextual Switching   NEW

What have we learned? To succeed and to prosper on the whitewater ride into the 21st century, multicultural organizations should hold a balanced workforce and a new management strategy. They should create a willingness-to-share attitude among the participants so that everybody would learn and develop core competence and the organization, itself, could learn and develop its distinctive core competence.

However, such proposition would not easily smooth out without dynamic actions of the aforementioned cultural and functional interfaces—that would be named *contextual switching* (Figure 78).

Basically, a contextual switcher (or a group of contextual switchers)'s main functions are:
1. To switch a cultural group's context to another or other cultural groups' contexts in order to smooth the team/unit/organization's motivational, interaction, visioning, and learning processes while tapping their diversity;

2. To generate/create a combining or intermediate or new context that would pull all the cultural groups to the common success.

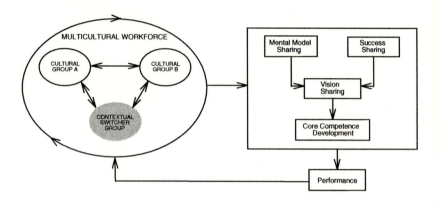

Figure 78: The concept of contextual switching (e.g., a case of three cultural groups)

Since learning process is a dynamic process, one could also expect that in the future, the other cultural groups would become potential contextual switchers.

Arguing for the need to continuously develop core competence through multicultural learning within organizations in order to cope with the new competitive environment, the present study suggests a strategic generation/creation of contextual switchers to facilitate the above mentioned strategy. A real commitment to such a strategy is essential for (1) managing a multicultural organization and (2) for developing its core competence.

As recognition of the importance of core competence as a source of competitive advantages will grow (Teramoto et al., 1993b), scholars and practitioners will emphasize on the ways in which each organizational member's core competence is shared, developed, and appropriated by his/her group and/or unit and/or organization for creating new core competence.

Organization gains and sustains competitive advantages by capitalizing on its strengths—its distinctive core competence. Being aware of that fact, organizations today are bracing themselves to meet this latest challenge through the bold restructuring of the economy and the rapid internationalization of business.

Chapter 7
CONCLUDING AND FURTHER THOUGHTS

7.1. Conclusion

One of the challenges often put to those who are doing research on multicultural management is, why retreat from classical "universals" into an area of great diversity and local contextual specificity? Just as macroeconomics can travel anywhere and be the same, is there no macromanagement theory and technology that can travel in the same manner?

The answer of this challenge is both yes and no. Yes, there are some universal management characteristics. Management is universally for example about organization, institutional analysis, motivation, establishing incentives, and implementing decisions. And no, not all aspects of these processes, when they are desegregated function in exactly the same manner in different cultural contexts.

The existence of techniques and concepts does not deny the salience of local culture variation. All languages have verbs a "universal" characteristic, but verbs vary in each language. All humans have circulatory systems too, but no surgeon performs surgery without detailed information (X-rays and laboratory work) about the specific characteristics of the individual patient. Although management as a science has some basic units of analysis, improving managerial and organizational performance requires considering the key impeding or facilitating learning, thus, core competence development; and these are culturally imbedded.

The intent of this book has been to develop an integrative and interactive model for an effective multicultural management and to test the related twenty-eight hypotheses through

empirical research.
1. Since all of the hypotheses on the effects of cultural distances have been accepted with both companies' data, one could fairly conclude that cultural diversity does really affect (positively and negatively) management and it should be carefully considered.
2. Also, the result reveals that sharing principle is a key for an effective multicultural management because:
    A) Many of the hypotheses on the conditions for an effective multicultural management have been accepted;
    B) The hypotheses subject of discussions could be accepted because the sample employees as a whole does support these hypotheses.
3. Moreover, since almost all of the hypotheses on the linkage between core competence development and performance have been accepted, it could be said that core competence development is positively correlated to performance.

Though the result of the hypotheses testing appears to support the validity of the theoretical model, it would be safe to mention that the existence of contextual switchers would be essential to smooth it out.

7.2. Implications

7.2.1. Theoretical Implications

1. Prior studies had a pessimistic view of cultural diversity because they hypothesized that it is difficult to coordinate and to manage multicultural workforces. This book however proposes an optimistic view of cultural diversity because it can bring many positive effects if the various energies, viewpoints, competencies, and so on are

effectively integrated.
2. Prior research that had the idea of various cultures integration (e.g., Hayashi, 1985, 1989) just considered and analyzed the issues of cultural diversity at the interaction process and at the performance level. In order to cope with the real and the practical issues, this book simultaneously considers the concept of motivational, interaction, visioning, and learning processes.
3. Recent works by Fiol (1991), Hamel (1990), and Reed and Defillipi (1990) provided insight into the relationship between organizational learning and core competence, but did not offer an integrative and interactive model. The model proposed in this book, in addition, integrates their insights and provides more precision in the explanation of the interrelationships.
4. Also, this book proposes the notion of multicultural learning and the concept of dynamic core competence (based on continuous multicultural learning and development of core competence). While there has been empirical research on competencies within firms, most were much earlier (e.g., Snow and Hrebiniak, 1980; Hitt and Ireland, 1985, 1986). There has been little empirical research on the notion of core competence as conceptualized here, the linkages between organizational learning and core competence, and on multicultural learning. Therefore, this study is intended as a pioneer of empirical research on dynamic core competence and their relationship to multicultural learning within the organization.

7.2.2. Managerial Implications

1. Up to now, as Cox (1993) mentioned, unbalanced power and unbalanced representation exist in multicultural organizations and, practically, these do hinder the smooth

of all the processes mentioned above. This book therefore proposes a redistribution of power through open and equal opportunity to succeed and to be promoted which, at the same time, would bring a more balanced representation at the management ranks. It is noteworthy to mention however that to balance power and representation is not attempting to replace one dominant group with another.

2. Up to now, multicultural organizations' strategies have generally been to avoid using diverse groups whenever possible or to homogenize them. This alternative is however no longer feasible. Managers cannot allow cultural diversity to hinder performance. They rather should be able to use cultural diversity as an asset since its potential benefits appear to be greater than its potential costs. This book therefore suggests an integration-oriented strategy (which values dynamic interactions among the various cultural groups) for multicultural organizations.

3. Up to now, multicultural organizations appear not to tap the power of cultural diversity because they are playing the game of homogeneous organizations, which relies on dependence on access to material resources and markets. To make the difference, this book therefore suggests that multicultural organizations will depend less than previously on the access to material resources and markets but more on organizational learning and core competence development. Indeed, organizations that could build dynamic and strong core competence would be able to take advantage of positive strategic opportunities to develop market power. In other words, they will likely gain important competitive advantages, which will produce significant market power. These organizations may be able to have more control over their environments and thus further reduce uncertainties.

7.3. Further Research

The further research is twofold:
1. To bring the findings to other countries/continents' multicultural organizations in order to gain a general acceptance.
2. Furthermore, the study expands the notion of cross-cultural interface management (from the work of Hayashi, 1985, 1989) via Ericsson Toshiba's case and introduces the notion of contextual switching to smooth out the aforementioned operationalized model. However, if a company would apply this new concept, the following question is worthy to be answered and developed.

"How can contextual switching be effectively performed?"

As recognition of importance of dynamic core competence will grow, scholars and practitioners will emphasize on the ways in which each organizational member's core competence is shared, developed, and appropriated by the group and/or unit and/or organization for creating new core competence.

References

Adler, N. J. (1991), *"International Dimensions of Organizational Behavior,"* Boston: PWS-Kent.
Albanese, R. and Van Fleet, D. D. (1985), "Rational Behavior in Groups: The Free-riding Tendency," *Academy of Management Review,* Vol. 10, pp. 244-255.
Allaire, Y. and Firsirotu, M. E. (1984), "Theories of Organizational Culture," *Organization Studies,* Vol. 5, pp. 193-226.
Amadieu, J. F. (1993), *"Organisations et Travail: Coopération, Conflit et Marchandage,"* Paris: Edition Vuibert.
Andrews, K. (1971), *"The Concept of Corporate Strategy,"* Homewood, IL: Richard D. Irwin.
Ansoff. H. I. (1965), *"Corporate Strategy,"* New York: McGraw-Hill.
Argyris, C. and Schon, K. A. (1978), *"Organizational Learning: A Theory of Active Perspective,"* Reading, MA: Addison-Wesley.
Aviel, D. (1990), "The Manager's Response to Cultural Barriers," *Industrial Management,* Vol. 32, No. 3, May-June, pp. 9-13.
Baker, W. E. (1994), *"Networking Smart: How to Build Relationships for Personal and Organizational Success,"* New York: McGraw-Hill.
Barney, J. (1991), "Firm Resources and the Theory of Competitive Advantage," *Journal of Management,* Vol. 17, pp. 99-120.
Belrose-Hyughues, V. (1979), "At the Origin of British Evangelization: The Dream of Madagascar," in Kent, R. K. (Ed.), *"Madagascar in History: Essays from the 1970's,"* Golden Horn: Berkeley.
Berry, J. W. (1980), "Social and Cultural Change," in Triandis, C.H. and Brislin, R. W. (Eds.), *"Handbook of Cross-cultural*

Psychology," Boston: Allyn and Bacon.

Bhagat, R. and MacQuaid, S. (1982), "Role of Subjective Culture in Organizations: A Review and Directions for Future Research," *Journal of Applied Psychology Monograph,* Vol. 67, pp. 653-685.

Block, P. (1987), *"The Empowered Manager: Positive Political Skills at Work,"* San Francisco, CA: Jossey-Bass.

Bosche, M. (1993), *"Le Management Interculturelle,"* Editions Nathan.

Brown, L. D. (1983), *"Managing Conflict at Organizational Interfaces,"* Reading, MA: Addison-Wesley.

Cannon-Bowers, J. A., Salas, E., and Converse, S. A. (1990), "Cognitive Psychology and Team Training: Shared Mental Models in Complex Systems," *Human Factors Bulletin,* Vol. 33, pp. 1-4.

Cannon-Bowers, J. A., Salas, E., and Converse, S. A. (1993), "Shared Mental Models in Expert Team Decision Making," in Castellan, N. J. (Ed.), *"Individual and Group Decision Making,"* Hillsdale, NJ: Lawrence Erlbaum Associates.

Carnevale, A. P. and Stone, S. C. (1994), "Diversity Beyond the Golden Rule," *Training and Development,* Vol. 48, No. 10, pp. 22-32.

Caves, R. E. (1971), "International Corporations: The Industrial Economics of Foreign Investment," *Economica,* Vol. 38, pp. 1-27.

Caves, R. E. and Porter, M. E. (1977), "From Entry Barriers to Mobility Barriers: Conjectural Decisions and Contrived Deterrence to New Competition," *Quarterly Journal of Economics,* Vol. 91, pp. 241-262.

Chandler, A. (1990), *"Scale and Scope,"* Cambridge, MA: Harvard University Press.

Collins, B. E. and Guetzkow, H. (1964), *"A Social Psychology of Group Processes for Decision-making,"* New York: Wiley.

Copeland, L. (1988), "Valuing Workplace Diversity," *Personnel,* pp. 52-60.

Covell, M. (1987), *"Madagascar: Politics, Economics, and Society,"* Paris: Frances Pinter Publishers.

Cox, T. H. (1990), "Problems With Research by Organizational Scholars on Issues of Race and Ethnicity," *Journal of Applied Behavioral Science,* Vol. 26, pp. 5-23.

Cox, T. H. (1991), "The Multicultural Organization," *The Executive,* Vol. 5, No. 2, pp. 34-47.

Cox, T. H. (1993), *"Cultural Diversity in Organizations: Theory, Research and Practice,"* San Francisco: Berrett-Koehler.

Cox. T. H. and Blake, S. (1991), "Managing Cultural Diversity: Implications for Organizational Competitiveness," *The Executive,* Vol. 5, No. 3, pp. 45-56.

Cox. T. H. and Finley-Nickelson, J. (1991), "Models of Acculturation for Intraorganizational Cultural Diversity," *Canadian Journal of Administrative Sciences,* Vol. 8, No. 2, pp. 90-100.

Cox, T. H., Lobel, S. A., and McLeod, P. L. (1991), "Effects of Ethnic Group Cultural Differences on Cooperative and Competitive Behavior on a Group Task," *Academy of Management Journal,* Vol. 4, pp. 827-847.

Cushner, K. and Trifonovitch, G. (1989), "Understanding Misunderstanding: Barriers to Dealing With Diversity," *Social Education,* Vol. 53, No. 5, September, pp. 318-321.

Denison, D. R. (1990), *"Corporate Culture and Organizational Effectiveness,"* New York: John Wiley and Sons.

Dierickx, I. and Coll, K. (1989), "Asset Stock Accumulation and Sustainability of Competitive Advantage," *Management Science,* Vol. 33, pp. 1504-1511.

D'Iribarne, P. (1986), "Vers une Gestion Culturelle des Entreprises," *Annales des Mines—Gérer et Comprendre,* No. 4, pp. 77-85.

Doktor, R. H. (1990), "Asian and American CEOs: A Comparative Study," *Organizational Dynamics,* Vol. 18, No. 3, pp. 46-56.

Donnellon, A., Gray, B., and Bougon, M. G. (1986), "Communication, Meaning, and Organized Action," *Administrative Science Quarterly,* Vol. 31, pp. 43-55.

Dorais, L. A. (1994), "Management of Cultural Diversity and The Public Service in Canada," *Optimum,* Vol. 24, No. 4, pp. 49-57.

Dosi, G. (1988), "Sources, Procedures, and Microeconomic Effects of Innovation," *Journal of Economic Literature,* Vol. 26, pp. 1120-1170.

Ebadi, Y. and Utterback, J. M. (1984), "The Effects of Communication on Technological Innovation," *Management Science,* Vol. 30, pp. 572-585.

Elashmawi, F. and Harris, P. R. (1993), *"Multicultural Management: New Skills for Global Success,"* Houston: Gulf.

Erez, M. (1986), "The Congruence of Goal Setting Strategies With Sociocultural Values and Its Effects on Performance," *Journal of Management,* Vol. 8, pp. 83-90.

Erlich, M. (1993), "Making Sense of the Bicultural Workplace," *Business Mexico,* August, pp. 16, 19.

Esty, K. (1988), "Diversity is Good for Business," *Executive Excellence,* Vol. 5, pp. 5-6.

Evers, H. (1991), "Optimizing the Use of Social Science Know-How in Development Cooperation," in Schönhuth, M. (ed.), *"Socio-Cultural Dimension,"* Eschborn, Germany: Deutsche Gesellschaft für Technische.

Fenelon, J. R. and Megargee, E. I. (1971), "Influence of Race on the Manifestation of Leadership," *Journal of Applied Psychology,* Vol. 55, pp. 353-358.

Fernandez J. P. (1981), "Racism and Sexism in Corporate Life," Lexington, MA: Lexington Books.

Fershtman, C. and Weiss, Y. (1993), "Social Status, Culture, and Economic Performance," *The Economic Journal,* Vol. 103, pp. 946-959.

Fiol, C. M. (1991), "Managing Culture as a Competitive

Resource: An Identity-based View of Sustainable Competitive Advantage," *Journal of Management,* Vol. 17, pp. 191-211.
Fiol, C. M. and Lyles, M. A. (1985), "Organizational Learning," *Academy of Management Review,* Vol. 10, pp. 803-813.
Fox. S. (1994), "Debating Management Learning: Part I," *Management Learning,* Vol. 25, No. 1, pp. 83-93.
Friedman, R. A. (1991), "Trust, Understanding, and Control: Factors Affecting Support for Mutual Gains Bargaining in Labor Negotiations," Paper presented at the annual meeting of the *Academy of Management,* Miami, FL.
Fukuda, J. (1988), *"Japanese-Style Management Transferred: The Experience of East Asia,"* London: Routledge.
Gaddy, C. D. and Wachtel, J. A. (1992), "Team Skills Training in Nuclear Power Plant Operations," in Swezey, R. W. and Salas, E. (Eds.), *"Teams: Their Training and Performance,"* Norwood, NJ: Ablex.
Galaskiewicz, J. (1985), "Interorganizational Relations," *Annual Review of Sociology,* Vol. 11, pp. 281-304.
Gersick, C. J. G. and Davis-Sacks, M. D. (1990), "Summary: Task Forces," in Hackman, J. R. (Ed.), *"Groups That Work (and Those That Don't): Creating Conditions for Effective Teamwork,"* San Francisco: Jossey-Bass.
Ghoshal, S. (1987), "Global Strategy: An Organizing Framework," *Strategic Management Journal,* Vol. 5, pp. 425-440.
Goodman, P. S. and Dean, J. W. (1982), "Creating Long-term Organizational Change," in Goodman, P. S. (Ed.), *"Change in Organizations: New Perspectives on Theory, Research, and Practice,"* San Francisco: Jossey-Bass.
Goodman, P. S., Devadas, R. and Hughson, T. L. G. (1988), "Groups and Productivity: Analyzing the Effectiveness of Self-managing Teams," in Campbell J. P. and Campbell R. J. (Eds.), *"Productivity in Organizations: New Perspectives From Industrial and Organizational Psychology,"* San

Francisco: Jossey-Bass.
Gosling J. (1994), "Interview With Henry Mintzberg (McGill University) and Sheila Forbes (Reed Elsevier)," *Management Learning,* Vol. 25, No. 1, pp. 95-104.
Graham-Moore and Ross, T. L. (1990), *"Gainsharing: Plans for Improving Performance,"* New York, NY: BNA Books.
Grandidier, A. and Grandidier, G. (1951), *"Histoire Physique, Naturelle et Politique de Madagascar,"* Imprimerie National, Vol. IV, Tome I: Madagascar.
Guetzkow, H. (1965), "Communication in Organizations," in March, J. G. (Ed.), *"Handbook of Organizations,"* Chicago: Rand McNally.
Hamel, G. (1991), "Competition for Competence and Interpartner Learning Within International Strategic Alliances," *Strategic Management Journal,* Vol. 12 (Special Issue), pp. 83-104.
Hamzah-Sendut and Datuk, T. S. (1991), "Managing in a Multicultural Society: The Malaysian Experience," *Malaysian Management Review,* Vol. 26, No. 1, pp. 61-69.
Harris, P. R. and Moran, R. T. (1987), "Managing Cultural Differences," 2nd ed., Houston: Gulf.
Hayashi, K. (1985), *"Ibunka Intafeisu Kanri," [Cross-cultural Interface Management],* Tokyo: Yuhikaku.
Hayashi, K. (1989), "A Comparative Analysis of Cross-cultural Interface Management: The United States and Japan," in Hayashi, K. (Ed.), *"The U.S.—Japanese Economic Relationship: Can It Be Improved?"* New York: New York University Press.
Hedberg, B. (1981), "How Organizations Learn and Unlearn," in Nystrom, P. and Starbuck, W. (Eds.), *"Handbook of Organizational Design,"* Oxford, England: Oxford University Press.
Hitt, M. A. and Ireland, R. D. (1985), "Corporate Distinctive Competence, Strategy, Industry, and Performance," *Strategic Management Journal,* Vol. 6, pp. 273-293.

Hitt, M. A. and Ireland, R. D. (1986), "Relationships Among Corporate Level Distinctive Competencies, Diversification Strategy, Corporate Structure, and Performance," *Journal of Management Studies,* Vol. 23, pp. 401-416.
Hofstede, G. (1980), *"Culture's Consequences: International Differences in Work-related Values,"* Beverly Hills, CA: Sage.
Hofstede, G. (1984), "The Cultural Relativity of the Quality of Life Concept," *Academy of Management Review,* Vol. 9, pp. 389-398.
Hofstede, G. (1991), "Cultures and Organizations: Software of the Mind," London: McGraw-Hill.
Hofstede, G. (1994), "Management Scientists Are Human," *Management Science,* Vol. 40, No. 1, pp. 4-13.
Huber, G. (1991), "Organizational Learning: The Contributing Processes and Literatures," *Organization Science,* Vol. 2, pp. 88-115.
Ishida, H. (1986), "Transferability of Japanese Human Resource Management Abroad," *Human Resource Management,* Spring, pp. 103-120.
Itami, H. (1987), *"Mobilizing Invisible Assets,"* Cambridge, MA: Harvard University Press.
Ivanier, D. (1992), "Qui Se Soucie Encore de la Nationalité des Entreprises?" *Annales des Mines—Gérer et Comprendre,* No. 28, pp. 42-53.
Jackofsky, E. F., Slocum, J. W., and McQuaid, S. J. (1988), "Cultural Values and the CEO: Alluring Companions," *Academy of Management Executive,* Vol. 2, pp. 39-49.
Jaeger, A. M. (1990), "The Applicability of Western Management Techniques in Developing Countries: A Cultural Perspective," in Jaeger, A. M. and Kanungo, R. N. (Eds.), *"Management in Developing Countries,"* London: Routledge.
James, K. and Snell, R. (1994), "The Need for Creative Enquiry for the Next Millennium," *Management Learning,* Vol. 25,

No. 1, pp. 5-10.
Jones, E. W. (1986), "Black Managers: The Dream Deferred," *Harvard Business Review,* Vol. 64, No. 3, pp. 84-93.
Judge, T. A. and Ferris, G. R. (1993), "Social Context of Performance Evaluation Decisions," *Academy of Management Journal,* Vol. 36, No. 1, pp. 80-105.
Kanter, R. M. (1983), *"The Change Masters,"* New York: Simon and Schuster.
Katzenbach, J. R. and Smith, D. K. (1993), "The Discipline of Teams," *Harvard Business Review,* p. 111-120.
Keys, J. B., Denton, L. T., and Miller, T. R. (1994), "The Japanese Management Theory Jungle-Revisited," *Journal of Management,* Vol. 20, No. 2, pp. 373-402.
Kirchmeyer, C. and Cohen, A. (1992), "Multicultural Groups: Their Performance and Reactions With Constructive Conflict," *Group and Organization Management,* Vol. 17, No. 2, pp. 153-163.
Klimosky, R. and Mohammed, S. (1994), "Team Mental Model: Construct or Metaphor?" *Journal of Management,* Vol. 20, pp. 403-437.
Kluckhohn, F. R. and Strodtbeck, F. L. (1961), *"Variations in Value Orientations,"* New York: Row, Peterson.
Kogut, B. (1988), "Joint Ventures: Theoretical and Empirical Perspectives," *Strategic Management Journal,* Vol. 9, pp. 319-332.
Kohls, L. R. (1981), *"Developing Intercultural Awareness,"* Washington: Society for Intercultural Education, Training, and Research.
Kotter, J. P. and Heskett, J. L. (1992), *"Corporate Culture and Performance,"* New York: The Free Press.
Kumar, K., Subramanian, R., and Nonis, S. A. (1991), "Cultural Diversity's Impact on Group Processes and Performance: Comparing Culturally Homogeneous and Culturally Diverse Work Groups Engaged in Problem Solving Tasks," *Southern Management Association Proceedings.*

Lachman, R., Nedd, A., and Hinings, B. (1994), "Analyzing Cross-national Management and Organizations: A Theoretical Framework," *Management Science,* Vol. 40, No. 1, pp. 40-55.

Larson, C. E. and LaFasto, F. M. J. (1989), *"Teamwork: What Must Go Right/What Can Go Wrong?"* Newbury Park, CA: Sage.

Laurent, A. (1983), "The Cultural Diversity of Western Conceptions of Management," *International Studies of Management and Organization,* INSEAD, Vol. 13, No. 1-2, pp. 75-96.

Levine, J. M. and Moreland, R. L. (1990), "Progress in Small Group Research," *Annual Review of Psychology,* Vol. 41, pp. 585-634.

Levitt, B. and March, J. G. (1988), "Organizational Learning," *Annual Review of Sociology,* Vol. 14, pp. 319-340.

Mackie, D. M. and Goethals, G. R. (1987), "Individual and Group Goals," in Hendrick, C. (Ed.), *"Review of Personality and Social Psychology,"* Beverly Hills, CA: Sage.

Mahoney, J. T. and Pandian, J. R. (1992), "The Resource-based View Within the Conversation of Strategic Management," *Strategic Management Journal,* Vol. 13, pp. 363-382.

Mandell, B. and Kohler-Gray, S. (1990), "Management Development that Values Diversity," *Personnel,* Vol. 67, pp. 41-47.

March, J. G. (1995), "The Future, Disposable Organizations, and the Rigidities of Imagination," *Organization: Articles on Organizational Future,* Vol. 2(3/4), pp. 427-440.

March, R. (1992), *"Working for a Japanese Company: Insights Into the Multicultural Workforce,"* Tokyo: Kodansha International.

Marmer-Solomon, C. (1989), "The Corporate Response to Workforce Diversity," *Personnel Journal,* pp. 43-53.

Marsick, V. J. (1994), "Trends in Managerial Reinvention," *Management Learning,* Vol. 25, No. 1, pp. 11-33.

Matsui, T., Kakuyama, T., and Onglatco, M. U. (1987), "Effects of Goals and Feedback on Performance in Groups," *Journal of Applied Psychology,* Vol. 72, pp. 407-415.

Maurice, M., Sellier, F., and Silvestre, J.-J. (1992), "Analyse Sociétale et Cultures Nationales: Réponse à Philippe d'Iribarne," *Revue Française de Sociologie,* Vol. 33, pp. 75-86.

Maurice, M., Serge, A., and Warner, M. (1980), "Societal Differences in Organizing Manufacturing Units: A Comparison of France, West Germany, and Great Britain," *Organization Studies,* Vol. 1, No. 1, pp. 59-86.

Maznevski, M. L. (1994), "Understanding Our Differences: Performance in Decision-making Groups With Diverse Members," *Human Relations,* Vol. 47, No. 5, p. 531-552.

Mazrui, A. A. (1992), "Development in a Multi-Cultural Context: Trends and Tensions," in Serageldin, I. and Taboroff, J. (Eds.), *"Culture and Development in Africa,"* Washington: Environmentally Sustainable Development Proceedings Series No. 1.

McCarrey, M. (1988), "Work and Personal Values for Canadian Anglophones and Francophones," *Canadian Psychology,* Vol. 29, pp. 69-83.

McLeod, P. L. and Lobe, S. A. (1992), "The Effects of Ethnic Diversity on Idea Generation in Small Groups," *Academy of Management,* Annual Meeting Best Papers Proceedings, pp. 227-231.

Meschi, P. and Roger, A. (1994), "Cultural Context and Social Effectiveness in International Joint Ventures," *Management International Review,* Vol. 34, No. 3, p. 197-215.

Nelson, R. R. and Winter, S. G. (1982), *"An Evolutionary Theory of Economic Change,"* Cambridge, MA: Belkap Press.

Northcraft, G. and Neale, M. (1990), *"Organizational Behavior: A Management Challenge,"* Chicago: Dryden Press.

Orasanu, J. and Salas, E. (1993), "Team Decision Making in Complex Environments," in Klein, G. A., Orasanu, J., Calderwood, R., and Zsambok, C. E. (Eds.), *"Decision Making in Action: Models and Methods,"* Norwood, NJ: Ablex.

Paillard, Y. G. (1979), "The First and Second Malagasy Republics: The Difficult Road of Independence," in Kent, R. K. (Ed.), *"Madagascar in History: Essays from the 1970's,"* Golden Horn: Berkeley.

Pearson, C. A. L. (1987), "Participative Goal Setting As a Strategy for Improving Performance and Job Satisfaction: A Longitudinal Evaluation With Railway Track Maintenance Gangs," *Human Relations,* Vol. 40, pp. 473-488.

Pedler, M., Burgoyne, J., and Boydell, T. (1991), *"The Learning Company: A Strategy for Sustainable Development,"* London: McGraw-Hill.

Pelz, D. C. and Andrews, F. F. (1978), *"Scientists in Organizations,"* Ann Arbor: University of Michigan.

Porter, M. E. (1985), *"Competitive Advantage,"* New York: Free Press.

Prahalad, C. K. and Hamel, G. (1990), "The Core Competence of the Corporation," *Harvard Business Review,* Vol. 68, No. 4, pp. 79-93.

Randolph, W. A. and Blackburn, R. S. (1989), "Managing Organizational Behavior," Homewood, IL: Richard D. Irwin.

Redding, S. G. (1980), "Cognition as an Aspect of Culture and Its Relation to Management Processes: An Explanatory View of the Chinese Case," *Journal of Management Studies,* Vol. 17, pp. 127-148.

Reed, R. and DeFillipi, R. J. (1990), "Causal Ambiguity, Barriers to Imitation, and Sustainable Competitive Advantage," *Academy of Management Review,* Vol. 15, pp. 88-102.

Rokeach, M. (1973), *"The Nature of Human Values,"* New York: The Free Press.

Ruhe, J. A. and Allen, W. R. (1977), "Differences and Similarities Between Black and White Leaders," *Proceedings of the American Institute for Decision Sciences, Northeast Division,* pp. 30-35.

Ruhe, J. A. and Eatman, J. (1977), "Effects of Racial Composition on Small Work Groups," *Small Group Behavior,* Vol. 8, pp. 479-486.

Rumelt, R. (1982), "Diversification Strategy and Profitability," *Strategic Management Journal,* Vol. 3, pp. 359-369.

Rumelt, R. (1984), "Towards a Strategic Theory of the Firm," in Lamb, R. (Ed.), *"Competitive Strategic Management,"* Englewood Cliffs, NJ: Prentice Hall.

Sabel, C. F. (1993), "Studied Trust: Building New Forms of Cooperation in a Volatile Economy," *Human Relations,* Vol. 46, No. 9, pp. 1133-1152.

Savage, C. M. (1990), *"Fifth Generation Management: Integrating Enterprises Through Human Networking,"* Bedford, Mass.: Digital Press.

Schein, E. H. (1992), *"Organizational Culture and Leadership,"* 2nd ed., San Francisco: Jossey-Bass.

Schein, E. H. (1993), "On Dialogue, Culture, and Organizational Learning," *Organizational Dynamics,* Vol. 22, No. 2, p. 40-51.

Schweiger, D. M., Sandberg, W. R., and Ragan, J. W. (1986), "Group Approaches for Improving Strategic Decision Making," *Academy of Management Journal,* Vol. 29, pp. 51-71.

Schweiger, D. M., Sandberg, W. R., and Rechner, P. L. (1989), "Experiental Effects of Dialectical Inquiry, Devil's Advocacy, and Consensus Approaches to Strategic Decision Making," *Academy of Management Journal,* Vol. 32, pp. 745-772.

Senge, P. (1990), *"The Fifth Discipline: The Art and Practice of the Learning Organization,"* New York: Doubleday.

Senge, P. (1992), "Mental Models," *Planning Review,* Vol. 20,

No. 2, pp. 4-16.
Shaw, M. E. (1981), *"Group Dynamics,"* New York: McGraw-Hill.
Shils, E. (1961), "Center and Periphery," in Polany, M. (Ed.), *"The Logic of Personal Knowledge,"* London: Routledge and Kegan Paul.
Simons, G. F., Vàquez, C., and Harris, P. R. (1993), *"Transcultural Leadership: Empowering the Diverse Workforce,"* Houston: Gulf.
Slepian, J. (1993), "Learning, Belief, and Action in Organizational Work Groups: A Conceptual Model of Work Group Learning." Unpublished paper presented at the 1993 Academy of Management conference, Atlanta, GA, May 1993, and paraphrased in Marsick, V. J. (1994), "Trends in Managerial Reinvention," *Management Learning,* Vol. 25, No. 1, pp. 11-33.
Snow, C. C. and Hrebiniak, L. G. (1980), "Strategy, Distinctive Competence, and Organizational Performance," *Administration Science Quarterly,* Vol. 25, pp. 317-336.
Sonnenberg, F. K. (1990), "The Professional and Personal Profits of Networking," *Training and Development,* Vol. 44, No. 9, pp. 55-60.
Spender, J. C. (1993), "Competitive Advantage From Tacit Knowledge? Unpacking the Concept and Its Strategic Implications," *Academy of Management Best Papers Proceedings,* August, pp. 37-41.
Sugden, R. (1986), *"The Economics of Rights, Co-operation, and Welfare,"* Oxford: Basil Blackwell.
Swieringa, J. and Wierdsma, A. (1992), *"Becoming a Learning Organization: Beyond the Learning Curve,"* Wokingham, England: Addison-Wesley.
Tang, S. F. and Kirkbride, P. S. (1986), "Developing Conflict Management Skills in Hong Kong: An Analysis of Some Cross-cultural Implications," *Management Education and Development,* Vol. 17, pp. 287-301.

Teramoto, Y., Richter, F., and Iwasaki, N. (1993a), "Learning to Succeed: What European Firms Can Learn From Japanese Approaches to Strategic Alliances," *Creativity and Innovation Management,* Vol. 2, No. 2, pp. 114-121.

Teramoto, Y., Nakanishi, A., Tsuchiya, S., Takeda, M., and Akizawa, H. (1993b), *"Gakushu Suru Soshiki,"* Tokyo: Doubunkan.

Teramoto, Y., Richter, F., Iwasaki, N., Takai, T., and Wakuta, Y. (1994), "Global Strategy in the Japanese Semiconductor Industry: Knowledge Creation Through Strategic Alliances," in Campbell, N. and Burton, F. (Eds), *"Japanese Multinationals: Strategies and Management in the Global Kaisha,"* London: Routledge.

Thomas, R. R., Jr. (1990), "From affirmative Action to Affirming Diversity," *Harvard Business Review,* Vol. 68, No. 2, pp. 107-117.

Tjosvold, D. (1991), *"The Conflict-positive Organization: Stimulate Diversity and Create Unity,"* Reading, MA: Addison-Wesley.

Tjosvold, D. and Deemer, D. K. (1980), "Effects of Controversy Within Cooperative or Competitive Context on Organizational Decision Making," *Journal of Applied Psychology,* Vol. 65, pp. 590-595.

Tjosvold, D. and Johnson, D. W. (1983), *"Productive Conflict,"* New York: Irvington.

Triandis, H. C. (1960), "Cognitive Similarity and Communication in a Dyad," *Human Relations,* Vol. 13, pp. 175-183.

Triandis, H. C., Hall, E. R., and Ewen, R. B. (1965), "Member Heterogeneity and Dyadic Creativity," *Human Relations,* Vol. 18, pp. 33-35.

Trilling, L. (1978), *"Beyond Culture,"* New York: Harcourt Brace Jovanovich.

Tung, R. L. (1994), "Strategic Management Thought in East Asia," *Organizational Dynamics,* Vol. 22, No. 4, pp. 55-65.

Vaid-Raizada, V. K. (1985), "Management of Interethnic Conflict in an Indian Manufacturing Organization," *Psychological Report,* Vol. 56, pp. 731-738.
Valette, J. (1979), "Radama I, the Unification of Madagascar and the Modernization of Imerina (1810-1828)," in Kent, R. K. (Ed.), *"Madagascar in History: Essays from the 1970's,"* Golden Horn: Berkeley.
Van Auken, P. M. (1993), "Supervising Culturally Diverse Employees," *Supervision,* Vol. 54, No. 8, pp. 11-23.
Watkins, K. E. and Marsick, V. J. (1993), *"Sculpting the Learning Organization: Lessons in the Art and Science of Systemic Change,"* San Francisco, CA: Jossey-Bass.
Watson, W. E. and Kumar, K. (1992), "Differences in Decision Making Regarding Risk-taking: A Comparison of Culturally Diverse and Culturally Homogeneous Groups," *International Journal of Intercultural Relations,* Vol. 16, pp. 53-65.
Watson, W. E., Kumar, K., and Michaelsen, L. K. (1993), "Cultural Diversity Impact on Interaction Process and Performance: Comparing Homogeneous and Diverse Task Groups," *Academy of Management Journal,* Vol. 36, No. 3, pp. 590-602.
Weber, M. (1977), *"The Protestant Ethic and The Spirit of Capitalism,"* London: Macmillan.
Weick, K. E. (1979), *"The Social Psychology of Organizing,"* Reading, MA: Addison-Wesley.
Weingart, L. R. (1992), "Impact of Group Goals, Task Component Complexity, Effort, and Planning on Group Performance," *Journal of Applied Psychology,* Vol. 77, pp. 682-693.
Wernerfelt, B. (1984), "A Resource-based View of the Firm," *Strategic Management Journal,* Vol. 5, pp. 171-180.
Wesseling, H. L. (1996), *"Divide and Rule: The Partition of Africa, 1880-1914,"* Westport, Conn.: Praeger.
Wilhelm, P. G. (1994), "The Influence of Mexican Culture on the Uses of US Management Theory in Mexico," *Cross-*

cultural Management: An International Journal, Vol. 1, No. 3, pp. 11-22.

Wilhelm, P. G. (1995), "Strategies for Integrating Gainsharing and Restructuring Into the Post-NAFTA Maquiladora Industry," *Cross-cultural Management: An International Journal,* Vol. 2, No. 1, pp. 33-42.

Williamson, O. E. (1985), *"The Economic Institutions of Capitalism,"* New York: Free Press.

Winter, S. G. (1987), "Knowledge and Competence as Strategic Assets," in Teece, D. J. (Ed.), *"The Competitive Challenge,"* Cambridge, MA: Ballinger.

Appendix: Indicators of the Selected Cultural Dimensions

Table A1: The chosen indicators
of POWER DISTANCE INDEX (PDI)

Indicators	Indexes
1. Members' Initiative	Tendency not to allow/desire group members' freedom and initiative at work.
2. Monitoring System	Preference for close supervision and/or authority at work.
3. Decision Making	Preference for an autocratic way.

Table A2: The chosen indicators
of UNCERTAINTY AVOIDANCE INDEX (UAI)

Indicators	Indexes
1. Rules & Procedures Orientation	Preference for respect and use of rules and procedures.
2. Monitoring System	Preference for use of authority and close supervision to ensure that the work is effectively done.
3. Nervousness	Tendency to be nervous or tense at work.
4. Risk Aversion	Tendency to avoid changes and/or failures.
5. Requirements & Instructions	Tendency to care about details and specificity.
6. Time Orientation	Tendency to care about time and to run after it.

Appendix: Indicators of the Selected Cultural Dimensions

Table A3: The chosen indicators of MASCULINITY ORIENTATION INDEX (MAS)

Indicators	Indexes
1. Needs	Desire for earnings, advancement, prestige, power, recognition, and personal achievement rather than working conditions, relationships, job security, and cooperation.
2. Nervousness	Frequent stress and nervousness at work.
3. Decision Making	Preference for individual decisions.
4. Gender	Tendency to think that men and women are significantly different.
5. Excelling Orientation	Desire for growth and excellence.
6. Time Orientation	Tendency to care about time and to run after it.

Table A4: The chosen indicators of GROUP ORIENTATION INDEX (GIND)

Indicators	Indexes
1. Needs	Preference for working conditions, relationships, job security, and cooperation rather than earnings, advancement, prestige, power, recognition, and personal achievement.
2. Decision Making	Preference for group decisions.
3. Group Thinking	Tendency to think in terms of ingroups and outgroups.

Appendix: Indicators of the Selected Cultural Dimensions

Table A5: The chosen indicators of SPACE ORIENTATION INDEX (SPA)

Indicators	Indexes
1. Monitoring System	Tendency not to like authority and close supervision.
2. Perspective	Desire for a higher-level learning.
3. Physical contact	Tendency to express oneself with physical contact.

Table A6: The chosen indicators of TASK ORIENTATION INDEX (TAS)

Indicators	Indexes
1. Needs	Desire for earnings, advancement, prestige, power, recognition, and personal achievement rather than working conditions, relationships, job security, and cooperation.
2. Excelling Orientation	Desire for growth and excellence.
3. Perspective	Desire for a higher-level learning.

Table A7: The chosen indicators of HUMAN RELATION ORIENTATION INDEX (HUM)

Indicators	Indexes
1. Decision Making	Preference for a persuasive way.
2. Contact	Tendency to show/enjoy affection and sympathy with physical contact.
3. Working Place	Preference for a crowded workplace.
4. Needs	Preference for working conditions, relationships, job security, and cooperation rather than earnings, advancement, prestige, power, recognition, and personal achievement.

About the Author

Rasoava Rijamampianina is a senior research associate at Hokkaido University, in Japan. He specializes and has published extensively in the field of multicultural management and organizational learning. His other areas of expertise include Japanese corporate groups, Japanese management, team building, motivation, audit, and accounting science.

Dr. Rijamampianina received his MBA from Otaru University of Commerce and his doctorate from Hokkaido University (Japan), in addition to special studies at the University of Antananarivo and Institut National des Sciences Comptables et de l'Administration d'Entreprises (Madagascar).

Former auditor at Delta Audit Deloitte & Touche and fluent in English, French, Japanese, and Malagasy as well, he has been dealing with many multinationals and local firms in Africa and Asia.

Printed in the United States
928100002B